Economic Systems

Economic Systems

ROLF EIDEM and STAFFAN VIOTTI

Martin Robertson

First published in 1978 by Martin Robertson & Co. Ltd., 108 Cowley Road, Oxford OX4 1JF

ISBN 0 85520 207 6 (paperback edition)
ISBN 0 85520 208 4 (case edition)

Typeset by Preface Ltd., Salisbury
Printed and bound by Richard Clay at The Chaucer Press, Bungay

Contents

Preface

This book is a considerably revised version of a textbook originally written in Swedish in the early 1970s. Since it has been quite successful on the Swedish market, we thought it worthwhile to try to reach a broader international audience. The main use of the book is, we believe, in first or second-term courses in price and allocation theory. It can then serve to give institutional solidity to the abstractions of the basic theory. The book can also be used in introductory courses in comparative economic systems.

We have tried to keep the exposition as non-technical as possible without losing the stringence of good economic analysis. It should be possible to read and understand most of the text with no previous knowledge of economics, but such knowledge – above all in price and allocation theory – will certainly facilitate the reading.

The Institute for International Economic Studies of the University of Stockholm has been our workplace during the preparation of this book. It has provided us both with a stimulating intellectual surrounding and a wonderful secretarial staff. We want to thank all our colleagues at the Institute and William Branson, Pavel Pelikan and Richard Portes for helpful comments on earlier versions. Edda Liljenroth, Birgitta Eliason, Ann Marie Soler and Caroline Burton have taken the heavy burden of transforming our handwritten notes into a real manuscript.

Rolf Eidem
Staffan Viotti

Foreword

The analysis of comparative economic systems is one of the most important and at the same time difficult fields in economics.

One reason is that theoretical and empirical analysis in economics during the last two centuries has concentrated mainly on *one* type of economic systems – decentralized market systems based on private ownership of the means of production. There are several reasons for this. Market systems are older types of economic organization and hence have been possible to study for much longer periods; the regularity of behaviour patterns is easier to pin down in systems with many agents, as then we can rely on 'the law of large numbers'; and the existence of markets, with agents with assertedly very simple targets (profit maximization and utility maximization), creates a certain type of predictability, or even 'laws', of behaviour. Moreover, societies based on developed market systems are, empirically speaking, usually much more 'open' politically than centrally planned systems, and hence easier to get information and make research about.

Another reason for the difficulties of studying comparative economic systems is that it is difficult to define the borders of the 'economic' system relative to other systems, such as the political and the technical systems, and to sort out the importance of historical and institutional factors.

A third reason, finally, for the difficulties of studying economic systems is that values and wishful thinking easily creep in. A usual consequence is, as pointed out by Rolf Eidem and Staffan Viotti in this short textbook *Economic Systems*, that models describing 'idealized' versions of one type of economic system are often compared with necessarily 'imperfect' forms of systems of other types that exist in the real world.

An important feature of the present book is the attempt to compare, as much as possible, 'comparable' things: models of one system are compared with models of other systems. Models of one system are also compared with empirical counterparts of the same system. But the authors wisely try to avoid comparing *models* of one system with *factual counterparts* to different systems.

After a short description of a simple, verbal model designed to represent decentralized market systems and centralized non-market systems respectively, the authors discuss three empirical counterparts – the United States, the Soviet Union and France. This analysis is followed by a more general discussion in the context of a broader perspective to economic systems, by looking at the interrelation between the economic and the political system and by comparing two main aspects of economic systems: (1) the degree of centralization in decision-making, and (2) the structure of ownership.

By looking at the historical time path of societies representing different economic systems, the authors can take a fresh look at the celebrated hypothesis about a 'convergence' between the economic systems in East and West. By way of a case study of Yugoslavia, the authors also illustrate some problems that are connected with attempts to change the economic system, and to combine public ownership with a decentralized structure of decision-making in the allocation of resources.

Owing to the chosen approach and to the simplicity of exposition, the book should no doubt serve the purpose of a very useful introductory text to the theory of allocation of resources and economic systems.

Institute for International Economic Studies   *Assar Lindbeck*
Stockholm,
October 1977

1. Introduction

In the United States, anybody – provided he has enough money – can buy shares in a corporate firm. These shares will typically give the buyer the right to receive part of the firm's future profits and to influence its policy. In the Soviet Union private citizens are not allowed to buy such shares – and rights. All the 'shares' of the Soviet 'firm' are owned by the state and cannot be sold out to individual people. So the Soviet citizen will have to put pressure on the state to influence its policy.

All this is probably well-known to most readers. It is only one of many examples of the fact that certain economic problems are dealt with in very different ways in different parts of the world. Additional, less well-known or conspicuous examples are easily found once one starts to compare accounting practices, contract laws (e.g. in the labour market), health insurance systems etc. in different countries.

An economic system can broadly be defined as the network of institutions and arrangements directed towards using scarce resources of a certain organization. The purpose of this book is to study in a systematic way different economic systems, to distinguish the fundamental differences and similarities between various systems, and to try to explain why a certain system is designed the way it is.

1

1.1   The National Economic System

The definition of economic systems presented above is broad enough to cover systems ranging from the single household or firm to associations of groups of countries like the European Community. This book has a more limited scope. It concentrates on the economic system of the *national state*. This means that we study the interaction between government, firms, households, labour unions etc. in the economic sphere. Only rarely will we look inside the so-called micro-units (firms, households) to analyse their internal economic system. This is not because we consider comparative studies of, for instance, the organization of firms uninteresting, but because we think that comparative studies of the economic systems of national states are particularly rewarding to begin with.

The economic systems of the advanced industrialized countries that will be the object of our study have a very complex and multi-dimensional character. There is consequently no approach to this study that immediately strikes one as the natural one to choose. A possible – and frequently used – approach would be to start listing and describing the institutions in various economies and in field after field make detailed comparisons of these institutions. The risk with this method is that we get completely bogged down in institutional details without being able to distinguish fundamental systems' similarities and differences.

1.2   Centralized or Decentralized Decisions?

To be able to focus on fundamentals we have chosen to view economic systems from a certain angle. The key issue in this book is to what extent *allocation decisions are administered by central state authorities or are taken by the micro-units (households, firms) independently of state authorities through a system of markets.* In other words, the basic question we are going to ask when studying the economic system of various countries is whether resource allocation is mainly *centralized* or *decentralized*. Allocation is taken here in its broadest meaning to include the allocation of inputs to sectors of production and the allocation (or distribution) of output to final users.

Economic theory provides us with the simple tools appropriate for an analysis along the lines just sketched. Typically economists work with models that are idealized simplifications of the real world. Skilfully used, such models permit us to focus on those aspects that are considered to be of fundamental interest for the specific study. They also provide points of reference helping us to extract relevant information from a complicated flow of empirical observations.

In chapter 2 we start the exposition by presenting two such reference models, representing the two conceivable extremes of allocation systems: a system of perfectly centralized allocation and a system of perfectly decentralized allocation. In chapter 3 these idealized system models are used as the point of departure in the study of three actually existing economic systems: those of the United States, the Soviet Union and France. The selection is made so as to give as broad a representation of conceivable system variants as possible.

1.3 CAPITALISM, SOCIALISM AND ALLOCATION

A reader interested in comparative economic systems may ask why there has so far been no mention of the terms 'capitalism' and 'socialism', so popular in studies of this kind. When properly defined, these terms deal with the ownership structure of the economic system. Capitalism implies predominantly private ownership of productive resources, while socialism means that those resources are owned by the state. In chapter 4 we discuss (among other things) the relevance of an approach based on ownership characteristics. It turns out that, if ownership is interpreted in a strictly legal sense, such an approach becomes rather empty. But with ownership defined in an economically meaningful way we would get a relevant alternative to the approach we have chosen, i.e. that of centralized versus market allocation.

The economic system represents only one aspect of the whole complex social network characteristic of a modern society. We may consider the economic system as working in a broad socio-political environment in continual interaction with other parts of the social system. In some fields this interaction is particularly important and decisive for an understanding of the development of the economic system over time. In chapter 4 we discuss these problems. The question of how a fundamental change in the political system will influence the economic system and vice versa is analysed. The well-known theory of convergence, implying that different economic systems are becoming more and more alike as they develop, is briefly presented and critically examined. Then, in the last section of chapter 4, a short economic history of Yugoslavia in the postwar period is told to illustrate all the complicated social interaction involved in the shaping of an economic system.

1.4 FALSE COMPARISONS

The study of comparative economic systems – if properly performed! – can provide much interesting and relevant insight. But history is full of examples of how such studies are made only for propagandistic purposes to show that the own system is the superior one. In the atmosphere of political and ideological confrontation between 'east' and 'west' many writers on both sides have taken great pains to paint their own economic system in as bright colours as the opponent system has been painted black. Economists as well as politicians have in many instances played the game of comparing ideally functioning models of their own economic system with other systems as they function in a less perfect reality.

In the final chapter we discuss the possibilities of making evaluative economic systems comparisons that do not degenerate into subjective value judgements or propagandistic statements.

Before we proceed it should be noted that this book deals with the economic systems of industrialized countries with an advanced division of labour and specialization. The primitive economy, characterized by little specialization and allocation systems based largely on the traditions and rites characteristic for many of the developing countries, is not studied. A satisfactory treatment of this big subject would simply not be possible within the limits of this book.

2. Two Theoretical Models of Resource Allocation

We will begin the study of different economic systems from the point of view of resource allocation by presenting strongly simplified, theoretical models of two allocation systems. These models represent two extremes: the completely _centralized_ and the completely _decentralized_ system. Of course, it would have been possible to base the analysis on alternative system models. We have chosen these particular models because they bring out clearly the two most important and fundamentally different principles of resource allocation.

The models might appear unduly abstract and far from real life at the first reading. Indeed, these shorthand models have been deliberately simplified to focus the reader's attention on basic principles rather than institutional details. The models have no real-life counterpart. They serve only as a background that can make the following discussion about resource allocation in the United States, the Soviet Union, France and Yugoslavia more systematic and comprehensible.

2.1 A MODEL OF A COMPLETELY CENTRALIZED ALLOCATION SYSTEM

In a system where resource allocation is completely centralized, _all_ decisions concerning consumption, investment and production are made by one central body at the macro-level. This central body, which could be characterized as an agency for economic planning at the government level, we have termed the central macro-level authority (CMA). The task of the CMA is to collect and rework economic information so that production orders can be issued to all enterprises. These orders should contain exact specifications concerning what factors of production (labour, capital etc.) should be used and in what quantities. Also, the enterprises get detailed instructions about all investments to be made. All the enterprises do is follow these orders.

The CMA also decides on the distribution of that part of production that has been earmarked for consumption. Goods and services are distributed to every single houshold or household member in centrally determined quantities through individual 'consumption coupons'. Like the enterprises, the households simply follow the instructions of the CMA

Complete Centralization – An Illustration

Let us imagine that it has been reported that the fishing waters of a certain country have become heavily polluted with mercury. On the basis of this information the CMA decides that for health reasons the consumption of fish should immediately be cut down. Orders are therefore sent out to fishery enterprises to cut down their activities correspondingly. At the same time, however, the CMA must see to it that the production of other foodstuffs increases, so that the total needs of food consumption are as well satisfied as possible despite the reduction of fish consumption.

Let us further imagine that the CMA at this point decides to increase the production and consumption of meat to replace the shrinking consumption of fish. Orders are now sent out to all meat-producing enterprises to raise meat production. But to make this possible more factors of production must be transferred to this industry. The CMA collects and works over all necessary information concerning the conditions of production in this industry. Also, it calculates the quantities of labour machines and land that are needed to achieve the planned increase in meat production. As far as labour is concerned, resources are obviously available in the fishing industry that could be carried over into meat production. If the necessary resources are not available in sufficient quantities in this simple way, a balance will have to be struck between the need for various factors of production in meat production and in other branches. Such considerations will lead to changes in resource allocation decisions made earlier. New production orders must therefore be sent out – and not only to meat-producing enterprises – with exact instructions concerning the changes in the inputs of various factors of production etc.

The Model Postulates Perfect Information...

In order to achieve, with no mistakes and delays, a reallocation of production and consumption of the type illustrated above, the CMA must have a great deal of information at its disposal. First, it must have all the necessary information about what waters have been polluted and to what extent, what kinds of fish have been particularly affected, etc., to be able to design the right orders for reducing production. Second, the CMA must know everything about the consequences for the national economy of a cut-down in fish consumption and also about the possibilities of substituting other consumption for fish (with due regard to tastes, needs for nourishment etc.). Third, the CMA must be informed about production possibilities in all the industries, which will somehow be affected by the necessary reallocation of production, in particular the meat industry: to what extent is labour really used to full capacity? What machines and instruments are utilized in different industries and to what extent can they be used in other lines of production as well? What fuel reserves are there? etc.

One can readily understand that the CMA needs a lot of information to be able to formulate exact orders to all the enterprises involved in the planned changes in production. But this is not all. The CMA must also see to it that the 'new' production of foodstuffs is distributed to all households in accordance with their preferences.

If the need for information is great in the case of such a limited reallocation of resources as the one illustrated above, it will, of course, be infinitely much greater when the CMA has to make *all* decisions on the allocation of resources in the *whole* economy. In a modern economy decisions must be made about tens of thousands of different products, which should be produced in certain desired qualities and quantities. Also it is the task of the CMA to specify how this should be done, that is to decide which of all conceivable combinations of labour, capital and raw materials should be chosen in tens of thousands of enterprises. Finally, the CMA must distribute consumption goods to millions of households in a rational way. All in all, this is a co-ordinative task of enormous dimensions.

In this model of completely centralized allocation it is assumed that the CMA has *perfect information* in all areas: about the preferences of the households with respect to consumption as well as work and about the production possibilities of the enterprises. On this assumption the CMA can avail itself of all the information *it* judges necessary to provide all enterprises with allocation decisions that are mutually co-ordinated or *consistent*. When these decisions are such that all foreseen needs (of both producers' goods and consumers' goods) fit in exactly with a corresponding set of centrally decided deliveries with no resources left over or missing, they are said to be consistent.

In such a system there is no need for money. The physical or quantitative detail instructions mean that all parties involved – enterprises as well as households – get the goods directly into their hands in the proper quantities. Consequently, money and prices have no independent role to play as a guide in the allocation process. It is possible that the CMA will want to use prices – e.g. so-called shadow prices – to describe the costs of constraints connected with different allocation alternatives, but this would be only for *internal* decision-making purposes.

. . . and a Perfect Consensus of Values

However, the mere fact that the CMA has perfect information and so is able to co-ordinate allocation decisions is no guarantee that the decisions are also reasonably efficient in the sense that scarce resources are used in the best possible way. What if the information fed into the CMA is false and thus not representative of the true consumption preferences and production possibilities? Clearly, allocation decisions based on such information, even if consistent, will not be efficient, since the information does not reveal the true costs or benefits of various allocations. It is assumed in this model *that* producers and consumers do not wilfully mislead the decision-makers in the CMA.

Now even if the information fed into the CMA is correct it might still be that some consumers or producers are disappointed with the allocation determined by the CMA in the sense that they got fewer goods or bigger obligations than expected. If, as a result of this, they do not follow the central instructions on allocation, efficiency will again be threatened. It is assumed in this model *that* consumers and producers strive to fulfil the orders and decisions of the CMA to the best of their ability.

When the consumers and producers act as suggested in these twin assumptions, it could be that they have complete confidence in the decision-makers of the CMA because the general values held by the directors and those directed are essentially the same (a common frame of reference, language, etc.). We call this underlying assumption that of a *perfect consensus of values*.

A Summary of the Characteristics of the Model

In the completely centralized allocation system (in the following referred to also as the CC model) all economic decisions – and by 'all' is really meant every single decision – are made by one central body at the macro-level, the CMA. Determining all consumption, investment and production activities in detail requires an enormous amount of information to become consistent. In this theory model it is assumed that the CMA can get all the information it thinks necessary to work out a set of consistent decisions – the assumption of perfect information. For these decisions to be efficient it is required (1) that the information fed into the CMA is true and (2) that the eventual decisions are carried out to the best of each person's ability – the assumption of a perfect consensus of values.

2.2   A MODEL OF A COMPLETELY DECENTRALIZED ALLOCATION SYSTEM

But who would take care of resource allocation if the CMA were simply removed from the scene? How, then, could the consumer and the producer possibly find their way among the innumerable consumption and production alternatives that are available in a highly developed industrial society? There is no central macro-level authority any more, that collects and works over information on a large scale and has such an overall view of the whole economy that it can make consistent allocation decisions. Obviously, consumers and producers must avail themselves on their own of the information necessary for their decision-making.

The Problem of Co-ordination in a System of Decentralized Allocation

The producers must know what goods and services the consumers want. They must also know what factors of production etc. are needed for the production of these goods and what production possibilities they have. The consumers, on the other hand, must know where to get the goods they want. However, they cannot get all the things they want. They need information that is comprehensive enough for them to be able to find that combination of goods and services which, given their disposable means, is in line with their preferences.

No doubt the problems of information in a setting like this are gigantic in a modern economy. All the same, we are inclined to regard the production and use of information in an economic system like that of, for instance, the United States, as a natural, everyday process. Is this because so much of the information is condensed in the prices that emerge in exchanges between consumers and producers? For, while we think of prices as 'costs' or 'necessary outlays', it is they that do most of the job of co-ordinating consumers' and producers' decisions.

Complete Decentralization – An Illustration

Let us return to 'the mercury pollution case' used above to illustrate the centralized model and study the corresponding process of adjustment in an allocation system where the role of the CMA is played instead by individual consumers and producers – and prices.

Through the mass media, the public becomes informed of the increased risk that fish are polluted with mercury. In consequence of this the demand for fish diminishes. At the same time consumers begin to look for different ways to replace fish by other types of food. Assume that they choose to a large extent to substitute meat for fish: the demand for meat increases, which in turn causes the price of meat to rise. This a signal to the producers that they could increase profits by increasing the production of meat. This, in turn, requires a larger input of factors of production (labour, machines, land, etc.). But where are these extra inputs to be had – assuming that the whole economy is working at full capacity (full employment, etc.)?

What happened in the fish market? The price of fish went down because the demand for fish fell off. This was a sign to the producers that catching the 'normal' quantities would no longer be as profitable as before. Many fishermen have therefore begun to look for other occupations that pay better. They find that the price of meat has gone up, which has made the meat industry relatively profitable. Consequently, many of them enter the meat-producing business either as entrepreneurs or as employees in already existing enterprises, thereby helping to satisfy the increased demand for meat.

The Role of the Price System in the Allocation Process

Thus, in the model of the completely decentralized allocation system presented here, the problems of information and co-ordination are solved by the price system replacing the central macro-level authority. In this model *all* economic decisions are made at the micro-level, by the enterprises and households themselves. The consumer himself decides in detail about his own consumption expenditures and also decides himself how many hours he should work. Likewise, the producer makes all decisions concerning the volume and com-position of production, investment, etc., on his own. Prices serve as the prime basis for such decisions. Since all economic agents involved base their decisions on one coherent system of prices, a simultaneous co-ordination of all decisions is in fact achieved without anybody striving explicitly for this.

Prices are formed in *markets*, where the sellers name the (minimum) price they want for their goods and services and the buyers the (maximum) price they are willing to pay. If the sellers start with a price that is too high there will be *excess supply* of the goods in question; unsold goods will pile up on the shelves. The price will now fall, making producers less eager to supply the goods in the market and consumers more willing to buy it. This will continue until what is called the equilibrium price is reached. At this particular price the market is said to be in equilibrium in the sense that all who can buy and sell at the equilibrium price can do so without the sellers getting any unsold goods left. The reader will have no difficulty going through the corresponding process when the starting point is instead a situation of *excess demand*.

If the price of a good falls, for instance because production costs have fallen, this indicates to the consumers that they can get more satisfaction out of their consumption expenditures by buying more of this particular good. In contrast, the price of a good increases if the consumers suddenly develop a very strong liking for it. This is an indication to the producers that it will pay for them to increase the production of this good (cf. 'the mercury pollution case').

The Model Postulates Perfect Flexibility of Prices . . .

Thus the prices formed in the markets function as signals to both consumers and producers. When the decisions of consumers and producers are such that an equilibrium price prevails in each market they are consistent. However, it may not be possible to reach a consistent solution if prices are sticky or immobile for institutional or other reasons. In this model it is assumed that prices in all markets respond so flexibly to changes in demand and supply that it is possible to reach a consistent allocation. We call this the assumption of perfect flexibility of prices.

. . . and Perfect Smallness, and Competition

As in the centralized model above, mere consistency in the decentralized economy does not imply that the solution reached is also efficient. Again in similarity with the centralized model, it is a precondition for efficiency that the decision-makers base their decisions on information that gives a true representation of the social costs and benefits associated with different allocations. By this is meant information as to what amount of resources have to be sacrificed or forgone to get a certain good. However, unlike the centralized model, it is not enough to assume that consumers and producers in the decentralized economy express their preferences and production possibilities in a truthful way, since this information does not – by assumption – go directly to the CMA. Instead it materializes in market prices, and they may give an untruthful representation of social costs and benefits for other reasons as well.

One such reason is that all the manifold and hard-to-measure effects of enterprise and household activities may not be registered through the price system, a possibility that is assumed away in this model economy. Another such reason is that a single enterprise could be so big relative to the market as a whole that it could influence the market price through measures of its own, a monopoly position being an extreme such case. Price-setting in such markets can be expected to give an unduly large weight to the interests of the leading enterprise, which will be able to set the price above marginal cost. But the marginal represents the true social cost, and so the price overstates the true cost. This is misleading to consumers and producers and makes allocation less efficient than it could be. The only way to avoid misallocation of this nature would be to make it impossible for enterprises to grow into market dominants and price-makers. In this model it is assumed that *all* sellers (enterprises) and buyers are so small relative to the market as a whole that none can affect the market price through measures of its own. Instead they regard market prices as given – they are price-takers. Such producers tend to choose a volume of production whose marginal cost is equal to the market price. As a result, by this assumption our model system provides prices that give consumers and producers adequate information about scarcities.

However, even if prices reflect social costs in an acccptable way, it cannot be taken for granted that enterprises are actually operating at their lowest possible costs. The assumption of a perfect consensus of values between planners and producers made in the centralized model makes less sense in this decentralized model, where there is no CMA! Instead, it is assumed that markets are characterized by mutual competition between sellers (enterprises). This means, for instance, that a seller (enterprise) who does not take care to produce as cheaply as possible – in the face of given prices – may have to go bankrupt. Conversely, he who does take care to reduce costs may enjoy increased profits from this, if only till some newcomer establishes himself in the market to share in them. Thus to achieve in the decentralized model what a perfect consensus of values brought about in the centralized model, the twin assumptions of price-takers' markets and competition is needed. We give these assumptions the joint heading of perfect smallness and competition.

The Role of the State in a Decentralized Economy

By assumption, there was no need for a central macro-level authority to co-ordinate allocation decisions in this decentralized model system. Instead, co-ordination was achieved through exchanges in the market between independent buyers and sellers. But such exchanges may not come about if buyers and sellers cannot agree to a common set of rules under which they can transact goods and services. Here is a role for the state. Jointly, buyers and sellers are assumed to set up a common institution that can promote market exchange by defining the 'property rights' of the goods exchanged and the consequences of a potential breach of exchange contracts. Also, the state has a role to enforce such rules, though it does not itself take active part in market exchanges.

A Summary of the Characteristics of the Model

In the model of completely decentralized allocation (in the following referred to also as the CD model), *all* economic decisions – and by 'all' we really mean each and every one of them – are made by the households and enterprises themselves. They base their decisions on prices that are formed in markets as a result of the interplay between buyers and sellers. When the co-ordination of buyers' and sellers' decisions through the prices has led to a situation where supply equals demand in all markets – equilibrium – a consistent allocation has been achieved. The more flexible the prices, the more likely it is that there will be consistency ('perfect flexibility of prices'). Allocation will be better the more nearly prices reflect social costs and the more enterprises (and households) take care to keep costs down. To this effect the twin assumption of perfect smallness and competition has been introduced.

3. Economic Systems in Real Life

We have chosen to study the allocation systems of the United States and Soviet Union because these two economies can be said to be representatives of a decentralized and a centralized allocation system respectively. Both these countries can be looked upon as illustrative cases, situated somewhere at the opposite ends of an imagined ordering of systems that exist in the real world, ranging from the least to the most centralized system. It will appear, however, that these two real-life allocation systems differ considerably from the CD and CC models. Between these two opposite extremes there is a great number of allocation systems, where simultaneously both centralization and decentralization are important. The case of France will be discussed in brief as a representative of these 'mixed' economies.

Every allocation system is rooted in history, which has produced certain ideas and ideologies about the best way to organize the country's economy. This applies to Soviet 'centralism' as well as to American 'decentralism'. As a matter of fact, it is surprising in many cases that old ideas and notions should still be so important in a world that changes all the time. In order to understand better how allocation systems work we will therefore take a look also at their historical backgrounds.

3.1 RESOURCE ALLOCATION IN THE UNITED STATES

The resource allocation system of the United States illustrates how a system where decision-making is decentralized could function

15

in real life. It is not self-evident that the allocation system of the United States is more strongly decentralized than any other of the so-called market economies, i.e. that the United States most nearly resembles the CD model. It is not possible – and probably not very rewarding – to make an *exact* ordering of different countries with respect to the degree of decentralization of allocation decisions in the economy as a whole.

Bearing all this in mind, we have nevertheless chosen to study the United States. An important reason for this is that this country has for a long time been looked upon as a kind of prototype of the market economy. American economists, business managers and politicians have, to a far greater extent than their colleagues in other market economies, emphasized the importance of, for example, 'free competition'. This 'competition ideology' makes the American economic system especially interesting.

A Sketch of the Background

The American Constitution of 1776 was characterized by a certain concept of freedom, namely the freedom of the individual from inter-ference by the authorities. This may be explained by the fact that most of the earliest settlers were people who had emigrated to North America because they were persecuted for political or religious reasons. In the nineteenth century immigration changed character. The immigrants were now mostly poor farmers who did not have enough land to cultivate in Europe; they were attracted to North America by the possibility of settling on the vast farmlands which still lay uncultivated. It was in this period that the so-called 'Frontier' spirit arose, as the pioneer settlers, through hard work and under harsh conditions, slowly pushed the frontier further west.

Economic Progress Through the Market System

In the first half of the nineteenth century the American economy was based chiefly on agriculture. In the second half of the century the economy was rapidly industrialized. By the end of the nineteenth century the United States was the leading industrial nation of the world. These striking results were achieved without much inter-vention on the part of the government. By and large, government restrictions on individual economic activity were insignificant. The pioneer spirit, which earlier was connected with the men who had broken new land, now characterized rising industrialists, many of whom have become almost legendary, e.g. Rockefeller, Morgan, Ford, etc.

Economic historians have pointed to the economic system as such in explanation of this rapid development. Production was mostly organized in a great number of competing enterprises, which were typically owned and controlled by individual entrepreneurs. All enterprises had to fight for their existence and only the best ones survived, without growing so large as to be able to manoeuvre their competitors out of the market to stave off competition.

This picture of the American economic system in the middle of the nineteenth century bears a strong resemblance with the CD model system. Also, this picture of the allocation system has been important as Americans have formed their ideas how an economy should be organized. Indeed, many Americans still consider this strongly decentralized allocation system to be the best. Such 'decentralists' like to stress the importance for economic progress of competition in production. Each and every individual should be able to make his (or her) allocation decisions on his own. According to this view competition between individuals will see to it that goods are produced as cheaply as possible in accordance with consumer preferences. It would therefore be an advantage for the national economy as a whole, if the freedom of action of individuals be as unrestricted as possible.

The Classical System and the Present One

However, if the typical American of the middle of the last century were confronted with the American economic system of today he would make a number of surprising observations. He would soon learn that not all resources are exchanged through markets, but that an entity called the public sector is also in command of huge resources for purposes like defence, education etc. Also, he would be able to read every day in the newspaper about innumerable disputes between the government on the one hand and enterprises and households on the other about what laws should apply, what laws should be introduced or abolished, etc. All this would be a far cry from the smoothly functioning markets of the classical system with no governmental interference in allocation.

It will be the subject of the next section to suggest an explanation of why the classical or ideal system was gradually transformed into the present one.

The American Economic System and the Model of Completely Decentralized Allocation

No doubt, the American economy can still be said to rely basically on the market mechanism for the allocation of scarce resources; the typical American household (or household member) decides itself, on the basis of the information provided by the price system, what goods and services it should buy. The individual member of the household is also in principle free to choose any career, and with certain restrictions to decide how much he should work. Normally, the individual household, is not in a position to influence prices to any extent worth mentioning through its own demand. By and large, wage rates also are influenced only marginally by the individual. The wage structure is mainly a result of the interplay between supply and demand in different labour markets and the negotiation between trade unions and employers associations.

Thus the role of the household in the American allocation system seems to agree quite well with the role of the household in the CD model.

Also, an overwhelming part of production in the American economy takes place in enterprises that make their allocation decisions on their own without any direct intervention from central authorities. These decisions are based primarily on the information provided by the price system. The enterprise decides what production goals it should aim at and how many workers of different training it should employ. It also decides what products should be supplied on the market and in what quantities. Thus, the firms in the American economy also seem to fulfil the basic requirements of the CD model.

However, although the American economy relies mainly on the market mechanism in the allocation of resources, there are many important differences between the American allocation system and the CD model. In particular, the very minor role that was given the CMA in the theory model has expanded considerably in the American economy. One illustration of this is the growing importance of government intervention by legislation to maintain competition.

*Restrictions on Competition, Anti-Trust Legislation and Natural
Monopolies*
One of the conditions for the decentralized market economy to
function well was that neither firms nor households could influence
the market price to any extent through their own actions. As far
as the American households are concerned this is a realistic
assumption. But for enterprises the picture is quite different.

Instead of consisting of a large number of small competing firms,
most industries in the United States are characterized by markets
with relatively few big firms dominating the industry. This type of
market is called *oligopoly*. In the automobile industry, for instance,
the three biggest companies had a market share of around 90 per cent
in the late 1960s. In the cigarette industry the corresponding figure
was an estimated 70 per cent. In addition to the big dominating
companies, there are often small-size firms which are typically rather
short-lived.

What is the reason for this concentration of firms? In what sense
can it be said to affect resource allocation in a harmful way? Finally,
what has been done against it in the American economy?

Why do firms tend to concentrate? Think of an industry where the
technology of production is such that very large production units are
required to achieve the lowest possible average cost. In an industry
of this kind there will not be a great number of small, competing
firms which respond to the price signals from the market. Instead, it
will be profitable for the firms to expand, and the fastest-expanding
firm will get into the most favourable position in the market.
Through exploiting such economies of scale this firm could put its
competitors out of the market and create a monopoly position for
itself. In such a position the firm will be able to determine itself the
price of its product (or rather to decide the preferred combination of
price and sales volume). Also, it will be able to stave off other firms as
they try to start business in this industry. True, these firms may face
no legal restrictions against going into business; but there are other
serious obstacles such as the very large capital investments that are
often needed to get through all the initial difficulties of a new and
unknown firm. Thus the explanation to these concentration or
monopolization tendencies is to be found in the existence of
technological economies of scale.

Why is monopolization harmful? In the CD model it was assumed that no single enterprise was in a position to affect the market price through measures of its own. All enterprises should regard the market price as given 'from the outside', as a piece of information from the market. Otherwise the enterprise could take advantage of its monopoly position and set prices that do not reflect the true social cost. Furthermore, it is competition between enterprises that forces them to strive continuously to keep down costs and prices, to find new better techniques and introduce new goods. It should be possible for an entrepreneur to launch a venture in an industry, where he sees good profit opportunities.

Anti-trust legislation – is it effective? In fact, in the United States there are, formally, no legal impediments for a person wanting to go into business on his own. However, because of the above mentioned economies of scale, there are a number of real obstacles to overcome. The tendencies towards monopolization in a number of markets and their detrimental effects on competition were observed in the United States already at the turn of the century. Here was a role for the state authorities to intervene in market allocation through legislation against similar tendencies. Since then such resistance has become a major feature of central government policy towards business. Its most important manifestation is the number of laws that have been introduced against restrictive trade practices, the so-called *anti-trust laws*. Thus, in order to keep up competitive conditions in the economy in spite of the tendencies towards large-scale business, legislation has been much extended in the United States in comparison with the CD model. In addition to providing the legal framework necessary for the smooth functioning of a market system, the CMA tries through the anti-trust laws to fight the tendencies towards monopolization of the business sector.

It is difficult to evaluate the importance of these laws in the American economic system of today. On the one hand, there are those critical of the anti-trust legislation who point to the fact that many markets are still characterized by various restrictions on competition. On the other hand, many cases of suspected restrictive trade practices are tried in court every year. However, the American anti-trust legislation can be said to have been successful in so far as there are today very few industries where one single firm dominates the market. Although American markets are not normally characterized by a large number of small enterprise 'units' like in the CD model, this does not necessarily mean that competition is weak. Even in oligopolistic markets with a few dominating firms there is always a possibility that new firms are set up in markets where prices give profits above the normal. In addition to this, many such markets, e.g. the automobile industry, are exposed to import competition.

Natural monopolies. In some markets economies of scale may be so predominant that it would be wasteful from the point of view of society not to have all production concentrated in one single enterprise. With production spread in a number of units average costs would become considerably higher. In such cases monopoly turns out to be the most appropriate type of market from the point of view of the economy as a whole. To prevent the monopoly firm from taking advantage of its position, the CMA intervenes and regulates the price and the profits. Some enterprises are also owned by the federal authorities. Typical cases in which a natural monopoly of this kind may be said to prevail are the gas, electricity, telephone and postal services. The enterprises in charge of such activities in the United States, and accordingly regulated by the federal authorities, are called *public utilities*.

The Very Big Corporations – Centralized Allocation in a Market Economy
Thus, we find in the United States several firms that are really very big. They deserve a special comment because they are so big that they cannot at all be said to agree with the small, market-responding enterprises of the CD model. Therefore, for a fully satisfactory analysis of the American economic system it is not enough to follow the flows of resources *to and from* these big companies; we should also try to get an idea of how resource allocation decisions are made *inside* these companies. Unfortunately, there is no room for any more lengthy discussion of the matter in this book. We shall have to limit ourselves here to stating that the problems connected with centralization and decentralization are important not only in the study of the resource allocation system as a whole, but also in any examination of decision-making processes within the big companies. Indeed, it might be rewarding to compare the resource allocation system or systems inside these organizations with that of, for example, the planning activities in the Soviet industrial sector.

Some of these big corporations are really giant ones. In the middle of the 1970s the 500 biggest American industrial companies were responsible for more than half of total sales and employment in mining and manufacturing. The 50 biggest among these had approximately half of the sales, and about 40 per cent of the number of employed in these 500 firms! In 1976 General Motors had a sales turnover of $47 thousand million and employed 748,000 people.

These giant corporations are most common in mining and manufacturing. Family firms and other small-scale business are becoming less important. Today they appear most frequently in the retail and other fields of the service sector. However, in retail trade there is also a tendency towards bigger business units such as chain-store systems.

External Economies as a Cause for CMA Intervention
An important prerequisite for the decentralized market economy to function in an efficient way is that prices really give individual decision-makers correct information about social costs. If relative prices do not reflect social costs, they give no proper guidance to individuals in their decisions on how to allocate scarce resources.

In the CD model it was assumed that all prices had this desirable property. In real life, however, it may be different. An important reason for prices in a decentralized market economy not to reflect social costs correctly is the existence of *external economies and diseconomies*. Such economies/diseconomies are said to exist when the activity of an individual household or firm produces gains/losses for other households or firms without this being reflected in market prices. Take as an example a firm that runs a factory emitting disagreeable smoke. Since the price of polluting the air is zero (or at least very low), the firm need not include in its cost calculations the inconveniences felt by people living or working in the vicinity of the factory. A true calculation of the social costs of the activity of the firm should of course include the external diseconomies. In a completely decentralized market system there is, however, no guarantee that all these costs will appear on the firm's bill.

Therefore, the CMA intervenes and tries to correct the distortions in the allocation of resources that would come about through prices not including external effects. In fact, there is nothing unusual about external economies. They are very much a common everyday phenomenon. However, in general they are so unimportant in scale that costs of intervening are not matched by the gains in allocation. To cite an example, surely no one would call for central interventions in the resource allocation process just because somebody has beautiful flowers in his window, which neighbours and passers-by may enjoy without having to pay for the pleasure.

Intervention through market legislation. In the example of the smoke-emitting firm, we could first think of the CMA influencing the market through various *legislative measures*. The CMA may legislate that air is not to be regarded as a free good for the firm. Instead, the firm must buy the right to pollute the air from those living and working near the factory. Or the CMA may legislate that firms are not allowed to use the kind of raw materials that cause the disagreeable smoke or that they must install certain cleaning devices.

What these measures have in common is that in principle they just add to the basic rules that we have seen to be necessary for a market to work and leave it to individuals to act on their own in that market provided they follow these rules. They are non-discriminatory in the sense that the laws passed concern all economic agents equally.

Intervention through subsidies or taxes. A second way to correct for external effects in a market economy is to let the CMA directly influence *prices* so that they will better reflect social costs. This can be achieved through various taxes or subsidies. In the case of the smoke-emitting factory the CMA could put a tax on the firm's production, corresponding to the social cost of polluting the air heretofore not included in the firm's calculations. With these measures, firms and households will still operate on their own in the market; the only thing that has happened is that the CMA indirectly influences the direction of consumption and production through its tax/subsidy policy.

The measures taken by the CMA to correct for external effects considered so far were measures intended to make the market system work more effectively. In spite of the more active role given to the CMA in correcting the effects of externalities, the emphasis is still on decentralized decision-making very much like in the CD model.

Direct intervention – through price controls or through replacing the market. In some cases the intention of the CMA to influence certain prices may lead to direct price *controls*. Prices are then not formed in accordance with the development of supply and demand in the market, but are set by the authorities. Although the individual households and firms are free to judge whether they should buy or sell at the fixed price, the price will not automatically tend to change if demand does not equal supply. It is up to the controlling authorities to make decisions about price changes.

With direct price controls, the CMA has put restrictions on the free working of the market. A further step is to *replace* the market as an allocation device by various administrative methods. In the example of the smoke-emitting firm we could think of the public sector taking over production and determining the level of production centrally in order to get the amount of air pollution deemed tolerable by the CMA

To this end CMA could set up its own production unit and produce the goods or services on its own through an administrative apparatus. But the CMA need not replace the market altogether, for there is a variety of methods by which the CMA may intervene with centralized decisions. For instance, after having determined the total volume of production, the CMA may contract private firms to do the job; i.e., the CMA goes out into the market and buys goods or services, the production of which is organized on a decentralized basis by individual firms. Next, the goods or services could be distributed to the final users (consumers/households in case of consumption goods, investors/firms in case of investment goods) either through the market or through various centrally organized rationing devices. In the first case, the CMA tries to set a price on its goods or services that will clear the market or at least give the users appropriate information about the extent to which they should buy these goods. In the second case, the CMA determines centrally how much of the goods should go to different users.

It is probably fair to say that in the American economy there is an inclination to try to use pro-market measures to handle problems caused by externalities, i.e. to try to make the market function more effectively instead of replacing it. But since the pro-market measures discussed above do not make the American allocation system differ in any important respect from the CD model, we touch only briefly upon their use in the American economy. To give an example, the public policy towards the environmental problems that have grown rapidly in importance during the last decades can be said to have relied mainly on pro-market policy-measures, i.e. legislation and tax-subsidy schemes.

There are, however, some important areas in the American economic system where the CMA intervenes directly because of considerable externalities. Since these interventions mean clear deviations from the theory model of complete decentralization, we treat them in more detail.

Primary and secondary education in the United States is available free of charge and is also compulsory. The CMA determines the total amount of resources to be directed to education, and schools and other institutions providing educational services are also usually run by the CMA. In other words, the production and distribution of education has taken over by the CMA through administrative measures. The market system is not used in this area. Education has very important external economies. Indeed, a basic, individual education is necessary for a modern economy to function. A man who cannot read or write is severely handicapped in most activities and also often becomes a burden to others. He will find it hard to communicate with others in their work and to participate effectively in the social process of decision-making. Education enables him to contribute more to production and also to act in general with greater social responsibility. This will be to the benefit of lots of other people.

Investments in *bridges, dams and roads* is another example of important external economies that have led to CMA interventions in the American allocation system. If a private enterprise builds a bridge or a road to solve its own transport problem, the bridge will often prove to be useful to a lot of other people as well. In theory, it is possible for the entrepreneur to charge a fee to all who make use of the bridge. In practice, however, enforcing payment for such services will often call for a sizable administrative apparatus. If it is feared that the administrative and other costs will not be covered by the fees, the bridge may not be built at all, even if it would be quite useful from the point of view of the whole society. Of course, the prospective investor could always try to increase the fee to have his costs covered. But then that would eliminate some of the users of the bridge, and again the firm's value of the bridge would turn out to be smaller than its value to society. For these reasons private enterprises cannot be expected to allocate resources into such production to the extent that would be motivated from the point of view of the whole economy.

In the American economy therefore the CMA intervenes and determines the *total* amount of resources to be invested in roads, dams and bridges. Unlike the case with education, the *construction* work itself is not centrally administered by way of direct physical allocation of resources. Instead, it is common practice that the CMA, within the frame of an earmarked sum of money, asks for offers from competing, private contracting companies. The company that finally receives the order will then handle the economy of the project quite independently – on the basis of the price system – within the limits set by the appropriation.

Finally, let us conceive of a private enterprise producing *basic research* services, and selling its product to other firms and to the authorities. Such an enterprise would most likely run into difficulties for two reasons. First, the results of basic research are seldom demanded directly by firms. Second, the results of basic research often benefit a number of other social institutions and organizations in an indirect and hard-to-measure way. To make a register of all the individuals and organizations (in a broad sense) that have benefited from some specified research findings, then to estimate the added, total social value of these, and finally to transfer the corresponding sum of money to the actual research firm seems very nearly impossible. Therefore the CMA intervenes directly in the field of basic research and allocates means for such activities. In this way the production of basic research services has become bigger than it would have been if all basic research had been initiated by individual firms in the market.

Collective Goods and Centralization

Defence is an example of collective good. Military defence provides the individual citizens with services in the form of increased security against foreign intruders. Is it possible to determine through the market what quantities of defence services are demanded by different households and then allocate them accordingly? It is hard to see how such an arrangement could be made practicable for the simple reason that it would not be possible to allocate the services produced by a defence establishment to specific individuals. If a country has a strong defence, all citizens will enjoy the greater security against foreign attacks that goes with it, irrespective of whether they consider this security valuable or not. This kind of services is indivisible and therefore cannot be especially destined, i.e. allocated to some households but not to others.

A method to determine what goods are to be considered as

collective goods is the so-called principle of exclusion: a good is a private good if he who does not pay for it can be excluded or shut out from the benefits of using it; if this is not possible, that is if non-buyers cannot be shut out in this way, then the good is a collective good.

Since collective goods clearly cannot be allocated via a price system, the CMA must intervene to solve these allocation tasks. In the United States the citizens decide through voting and via Congress the total amount of resources to be spent on defence. The costs are covered by taxes and each and every citizen shares in the services produced by the defence organization.

Although the total expenditures to be spent on defence are determined centrally by the CMA, the market system is partly used in the various activities producing defence services. For the delivery of weapon systems and other kinds of military equipment, the CMA usually enters into contracts with private firms on the market, accepting the bids that seem economically most favourable.

There are many other public goods than defence, although the latter is today the 'largest' public good in the American economy. Others worth mentioning are law courts and public administration, police and fire protection.

The Central Macro-level Authority
In the foregoing we have spoken of the CMA as if it were one solid decision-making unit. In reality the field of activities of the CMA – the public sector – is so large and diverse that we find a number of different, decision-making authorities at various levels. We shall now take a closer look at these, i.e. at the structure and organization of the public sector in the United States.

The United States is a federal nation, consisting of fifty member states, which are in turn divided into local districts. The federal government and its legislative assembly, Congress, have a decisive influence in a number of economic or political questions of national importance such as the allocations to defence and space research and social security schemes of various kinds. State governments and local authorities are instead in charge of tasks like education, police and fire protection, all local facilities (roads, etc.) and welfare (see table 3.1).

Federal expenditures are almost twice as large as the combined total of state and local expenditures. Also, the federal government

Table 3.1 *Federal v. state—local expenditures by function in the United States, 1974*

Federal		State and local	
	$000,000,000		$000,000,000
National defence	79	Education	75
Income security	84	Highways	19
Commerce and		Public assistance	25
transportation	13	Police and fire	
Interest on public		protection	10
debt	22	Health and hospitals	16
Veterans' benefits	13	Sanitation and	
General science, space,		housing	9
and technology	4	Other (administration,	
Health	22	etc.)	45
Education	12		199
Agriculture	2		
Natural resources,			
environment and			
energy	7		
International affairs	4		
Law enforcement and			
justice	3		
General government	3		
	268		

Source: *National Income and Product Account*, US Department of Commerce.

contributes sizable sums to the budgets of the regional authorities. However, the government in Washington cannot specify in detail how all these allocations should be used. As a matter of fact, state, and to a certain extent also local, authorities have considerable leeway in allocating federal means. In many cases one may speak of conflicting interests between the different administrative levels, above all between the federal and state governments.

The CMA and Centralized Allocation in the US Economy
The public sector obviously plays an important role in the American economic system. But to what extent do CMA activities actually mean a move from a decentralized market system towards a centrally administered system?

CMA intervention through the budget. If we add all federal and state/local expenditures and relate the sum to the gross national product (GNP), we get a first indicator of the importance of the public sector in the American economy. In 1971 public expenditures equalled nearly 30 per cent of the American GNP. This indicator of the importance of the public sector is, however, not very relevant for our purposes. It does not tell us to what extent various types of public expenditures really imply direct central interventions in the allocation system, i.e. a divergence from the CD model.

In the first place, roughly one-fourth of public expenditures (cf. table 3.2) consists of *transfer payments*, i.e. redistribution of money primarily to households. In general, the households are free to dispose of such means as they themselves see fit. Thus the transfer expenditures do not affect the degree of centralization in economic decision-making.

Second, there are several fields of public expenditures, where these are not directly related to any corresponding 'public' production. The CMA only determines the general direction of production and then enters different markets to purchase goods and services from private enterprises. Military equipment and the construction of roads and bridges are cases in point. As seen from table 3.2, only about *half* of the public expenditures, excluding transfer payments, goes to pay for production that is directly *administered* by the CMA. Typical such activities are teaching services, defence services, and the services of policemen and public administrators.

In a similar way one could ask to what extent public goods and services are allocated to the final users through administrative

Table 3.2 *Expenditure in the public sector in the United States, 1974*

	$000,000,000	%
Purchases of goods and services	304	67
Government employees	163	36
Purchases from business	141	31
Transfer payments (including interest on public debt)	151	33
	455	100

Source: *National Income and Product Account*, US Department of Commerce.

methods and to what extent the market system is used. In the case of collective goods these cannot by their nature be allocated via prices, but in all other cases there is in principle an option of which method to rely upon. As we have seen, basic education is allocated to all citizens on a compulsory basis free of charge, while prices are often used to allocate and finance the services generated by public roads and bridges.

CMA intervention through legislation and regulation. To look only at the aggregate budget of the public sector does not give us the whole picture of the influence of the CMA over the allocation process. There are several measures taken by the CMA that have an important impact on the economy, but are not included in the budget figures. To recapitulate some measures already accounted for, the CMA may influence prices in a market to encourage or discourage the consumption or production of certain goods. The weaker form of such interventions is the use of taxes and subsidies, which leads to changes in allocation through changes in relative prices but without interfering with the working of the market system. The stronger form of intervention is direct regulations above all on prices in a market. Prices are then no longer free to adjust according to demand and supply, but are regulated by some central authority. Important fields with strong elements of market regulations are housing and agriculture. Banking and insurance are other examples where regulations play an important role.

Through legislative measures (other than direct market regulations) the CMA can also influence the allocation of resources. Through changes in legislation the CMA affects the general framework for individual decision-making. Previously we discussed anti-trust legislation in some detail. Another field of rapidly growing importance is that of consumer protection legislation.

CMA intervention through stabilization policy. So far the analysis of the American economic system has dealt with how resources are allocated via relative prices, which may or may not need to be corrected by the CMA. All the while it has been (implicitly) assumed that *all* resources are actually put to use; indeed, in the CD model it was assumed that prices were perfectly flexible so that the allocation problem was always given a *consistent* solution in the sense that all firms and households who wanted to transact goods or labour could do so without ever having to face, say, excess supply of goods – or of labour, i.e. unemployment. What price level the individual market prices added up to – and if it changed – did not enter into the analysis at all.

In real life, of course, it is a well-known fact that the decentralized market economy of the United States has not been able to make sure – through the co-ordination of independent firm and household decisions via the price system – that there is always full employment and a stable price level. Here, again, has been an opportunity for the state authorities to try and improve capacity utilization and price stability. Such so-called *stabilization policy* is perhaps the most conspicuous and generally debated kind of CMA policy in the United States. It is the use of monetary and fiscal policy measures to influence, in a stabilizing manner, economic aggregates such as the general level of employment and rate of capacity utilization and the rate of inflation.

Since the Great Depression in the 1930s an active stabilization policy has been an important feature of the American economy. Naturally, it influences the allocation of resources in the United States. But the main purpose of stabilization policy is to stabilize the economy over the business cycle, not to change the resources allocation. It also relies mainly on measures that influence the economy in a very general, non-discriminatory way, without favouring any particular sectors or branches. Monetary policy, for instance, works through changes in interest rates and credit conditions that in principle influence all firms and households equally in their investment and savings decisions.

How the CMA Makes Its Economic Decisions
What we have termed the CMA is obviously a very complex body in the United States, with a wide range of activities and responsibilities tied to it. What can be said about the decision-making process *within* the CMA? To illustrate this issue we turn to a brief description of the budgetary process in the United States. Although we will concentrate on the federal budget, the basic elements of the process are not too different for state and local budgets.

Formally, public decisions on the allocation of resources are made collectively in the United States, through Congress. However, before the final version of the proposed budget is presented for voting it will have gone through a long process of decision-making. It is true that the fiscal year starts on 1 July, but the preparations begin one year in advance, when all ministries and committees start formulating preliminary action programmes. These proposals are then given a comprehensive check-up by the budget office of the President to see that they are in agreement with the general directives on the sum total of public expenditures and the economic policies formulated by the President. Then the ministries and committees work out their budgetary proposals in detail and send them again to the budget office. Here the different proposals are weighed against each other to establish which fields should be given priority and which should not. These deliberations normally result in reductions of the total sum of expenditures. In January the budget proposal *in toto* is put before Congress, where it is debated in a number of committees until summer, when a final version is decided upon.

It is obvious then, that public decisions on resources allocation are made within an extensive and intricate administrative apparatus. It is difficult to tell where in this huge body the most important decisions are made. It seems likely that this should be in central government offices and at the 'presidential' weighing-up of the different sub-budgets, since here is where the knowledge of the issues at hand is really concentrated. However, one should not overlook the importance of Congress itself, especially in questions of a more general nature like, for example, the size of defence allocations.

The Role of the Public Sector in the Twentieth Century
Typical representatives of the American economic ideology have traditionally held the view that interventions by the authorities should be reduced to a minimum, namely law and order, public administration and defence. The private business sector should be left to run production on its own.

In the foregoing paragraphs we have pointed to the fact that the importance of the public sector has increased very rapidly in the twentieth century. However, if one takes a closer look at the fields of public activities of today it is clear that they are still to a very large extent restricted to areas that have long been considered particularly suitable for public endeavours. Compared with the situation in Europe, the public activities in the field of social security arrangements are relatively less pronounced in the United States. Health insurance, unemployment insurance and pensions are still mainly handled by private firms. A similar situation prevails in large parts of the educational system.

The more or less continuous expansion of the pubiic sector in the United States has probably served to lessen somewhat the aversion on the part of many Americans against public interventions in resources allocation. However, it would hardly be an overstatement to say that the typical American would still hold out a strongly decentralized, competitive economy as the ideal system.

Summary

We chose to study the United States because it has long been regarded as the 'pioneer' of market allocation. But the present economic system of the United States differs in important respects from the classical, typified here by the CD model.

First, as a result of technological economies of scale or for other reasons some firms may grow so big in the market that competition peters out. To uphold competition, state or central macro-level authority intervenes through market legislation (anti-trust laws); in certain instances the CMA regulates production more directly (natural monopoly).

Second, as a result of external economies and diseconomies, the 'pure' market must be supplemented through certain state measures. Through market legislation or price regulation (taxes/subsidies) the CMA can work to expand or reduce production or consumption over and above what the market alone achieves. In certain cases (e.g. primary and secondary education) the CMA takes over production and replaces the market.

Third, collective goods (e.g. defence) make centralization through the CMA necessary. This is because such goods cannot be produced for exclusive, individual consumption and so cannot be allocated via a price system.

The central macro-level authority thus influences the American economy in a number of ways: through legislation and regulation, and production and stabilization policy. Much of this influence is visible in the federal budget, but one should be careful to note what items on the budget affect the degree of centralization of decision-making. Many, like transfer payments, do not.

3.2   RESOURCE ALLOCATION IN THE SOVIET UNION

The allocation system of the Soviet Union seems to be the closest approximation of the model system with completely centralized resources allocation – at least to our knowledge. True, the resources allocation system in China is also of the centralized type, but here regional self-government seems to have developed much more than in the Soviet Union. In addition to this, the level of economic development is low in China, which would complicate a comparison with the United States or France. This last argument applies as well for highly centralized economies such as those of Albania and North Korea. Also, the information available on these economies is very meagre, whereas our knowledge of the Soviet economic system has improved considerably over the years. An additional reason for studying the Soviet Union is that this was the pioneer centralized economy and as such the model for many others.

A Sketch of the Background

How, then, should one explain that in the Soviet Union – in a world of capitalist, decentralized market economies – towards the end of the 1920s an altogether different economic system was introduced, based on state ownership of the means of production and with a centralized allocation of resources? To be sure, there is no fully satisfactory answer to that question; one cannot hope to get all historical coincidences in proper perspective. However, two fundamental factors stand out quite clearly in explanation of the final 'choice of system'. We have in mind, first, the general economic, social and political situation in Europe during the latter part of the nineteenth and the beginning of this century and the socialist critique against it; second, the particular Soviet problems and ideas of 1917 and the following ten years.

The industrial revolution in Europe in the nineteenth century certainly brought about a tremendous increase of commodity production. However, the abrupt and sweeping changes of a society, which had been highly stationary for long periods, also brought about strong social tension. The contrasts between rich and poor were particularly glaring in the big cities.

Karl Marx and his fellow critics embitteredly described the failures of the capitalist system, primarily in western Europe. Social injustice was said to be outrageous in many places. An overwhelming majority of the people were poor and had a miserable income, while a small number of capitalists were conspicuously wealthy. Workers were often forced to work recklessly hard, general working conditions were bad and, worst of all, the employed were in no position to put pressure on the employers to improve the worker's lot. Child labour was used in great numbers in hard factory work; for most of the children the chances to get a proper education were remote, while the fortunate few were of rich families. The wage-earners were heavily dependent on the factory-owner for their income; there was no unemployment insurance. In the eyes of Marx the root of all this evil was the capitalist system itself, which allowed individual capital-owners to hire other people to work in their private factories.

More than anything else, it seems to have been Marx's critical ideas that provided the leaders of the Russian Revolution with the underpinnings for their political and economic ideologies. In 1917 Lenin and the Bolsheviks seized power in Russia. It was their stated intention to create a new economic system that was of socialist nature. But what should it look like and how should it be brought about? Marx had not been very specific on these issues, since he devoted most of his energies to the study of the capitalist system. However, on one particular issue there seems to have been little hesitation among the revolutionary leaders, namely that private ownership of the means of production should be abolished. By transferring the means of production into its own hands, the state would automatically rid the private capitalists of their power. Since the means of production would then be owned jointly by each and every inhabitant, the people themselves would be in a position to run production and there would no longer be any conflict of interests between capitalists and workers. They would be one and the same, and so there would be no more exploitation. The former employers were to be replaced by managers appointed by state authorities. The latter would be placed under workers' control as a safeguard against bullying and arbitrariness in the old capitalist style.

Experiments and Tactics in the 1920s

At the time of the revolution Lenin and the other leaders seem to have taken a rather simplified view of the problem of resources allocation. In the first years following the revolution an attempt was made at a speedy centralization of decision-making in large parts of the economy – the so-called 'war communism'. This experience demonstrated vividly that the allocation problems were much more complicated than expected.

Lenin eventually concluded that, in the prevailing situation, it was impossible to replace altogether the market mechanism and the market system by central directives. The problems of information and co-ordination threatened to become insurmountable. Also, most of the new men in charge were very little versed in the techniques of planning.

These seem to have been the basic reasons why Lenin changed policies in the beginning of the 1920s. The new line, often referred to as the New Economic Policy, NEP, meant a change-over to a much *more* decentralized allocation system than that under 'war communism'. However, the state authorities retained control over some vital parts of the economy such as the banking system and the administration of foreign trade licences.

Arbitrariness and Stagnation through the Market Economy

However, the mere transfer of the ownership of the means of production from the old capitalists to the people, i.e. to some government body trusted to represent the people, did not by itself give the new rulers much guidance as to how production and exchange should be organized. Today we know by experience – Rumania and Yugoslavia, say – that resources allocation may be organized on both centralized and decentralized patterns, where the means of production are collectively owned. This the Bolshevik commissars could not know, for obvious reasons. Even worse, at the time of the Revolution there was little organized knowledge in the world about alternative models of allocation. With the exception of some heroic attempts to describe, say, the theoretical problem of central planning, it was around the market economy and its problems that research had centered. What should the commissars think of the market economy, i.e. of giving their allocation problem a decentralized solution? How could their thinking be expected to be modified by the knowledge that there existed no worked-out alternative? To return to the Marxist critique of the capitalist society it is probably right to say that here the market system was seen as a natural complement to the order of capitalist ownership of the means of production. However, in Marx there is also some 'independent' criticism of the market economy as such, which is said to be characterized by – to borrow a term of frequent Soviet textbook usage – 'anarchy', i.e. by more or less unpredictable and arbitrary results in terms of production and distribution. Most likely the revolutionary leaders basically favoured this interpretation of the market system and so to do away with it somehow.

Now if it had been believed in Russia as in the United States that the market economy, for all its arbitrariness, was an effective order for economic development, the commissars might have had second thoughts about this. But there was little in Russia's economic history that asserted the growth abilities of the market economy. True, there were periods of accelerated development from 1890 outwards, but they failed by far to bring Russia anywhere near the development level of, say, England or Germany at the time of the First World War. So, in contrast to the United States, the decentralized, market economy was seen to entail stagnation rather than progress.

The commissars, then, had at least two good reasons to replace the market economy. But with what? To avoid arbitrariness an overview was needed. Expansion, in turn, required mobilization and deployment of resources according to national rather than individual priorities. Both suggested a more centralized allocation system than the old. But how centralized and how soon?

In order to deter potential intruders, military strength had to be increased. This in turn necessitated a speedy increase in investments, above all in the so-called heavy industry (exploitation of raw materials, energy production and other branches of industry). This required in turn that the increase in consumption be restrained. The growth of investment goods production in the cities would be financed largely through central requisitions from the countryside. Through forcible *collectivization* agriculture would be placed under central control. In leading quarters there was little confidence in a willingness to co-operate on the part of the peasantry, whose general consensus of values with the party leadership in Moscow was believed to be rather narrow.

For the leaders of the Communist Party the overriding goal was to stay in power. In the prevailing situation the party leadership needed considerable freedom of action to be able to carry out their ambitious plans and simultaneously consolidate their political position. A centralized system of allocation was thought to be most readily compatible with the freedom of action required.

The Definitive Choice: Centralization
The New Economic Policy was successful in terms of its limited targets. It helped restore production to prewar levels reasonably quickly and also gave the commissars some time to think about industrialization policies and systems choice. However, since the improvements in living conditions through the NEP provided a more stable ground for social experiments in allocation modelling, it is somewhat surprising that this policy was discontinued already in 1928, in particular as no new allocation system seems to have been thought out and agreed upon at the time.

When, instead of continuing or gradually modifying the NEP, an entirely new allocation system was grafted on to the Soviet economy, this had to do more with developments abroad than at home. In particular it became increasingly clear towards the end of the 1920s that the European socialist revolutions that the Bolshevik leaders had hoped for would never materialize. Encircled by enemy capitalist states, the Soviet Union was to try and carry out 'socialism in one country', relying nearly entirely on its own resources for economic development.

Thus, the centralized allocation system eventually chosen may have been chosen largely because of its reallocative ability. In the foregoing paragraphs two other aspects were referred to that the system's architects will also have considered, i.e. how to avoid the arbitrariness and how to put an end to the economic stagnation that they associated with the market economy. The urgency of the political situation around 1930 may have caused these latter to be given less weight in the choice of allocation system than originally intended. It is important to recognize this when the Soviet economic system is criticized: not only was the step to introduce a centralized allocation system largely a step into the unknown; it was also made in great haste.

The Centralized Alternative
It was said above about the United States that the experience of rapid economic growth was associated with the market economy and so this allocation system became an ideal. Since there was no solid experience at all of centralized allocation systems around 1930, this allocation model could not become an ideal in the same sense. It was looked upon as the natural alternative to the market system, but not as an *ideal*. Indeed, we do not know even today which ideal system the Soviet leaders have been striving for!

Also, any visitor to the Soviet Union today would make a lot of observations that would clearly be out of line with what one would have expected to see on the basis of the CC model. He or she would see consumers crowding in shops buying price-tagged goods with money much like in the market economy. The visitor might even see business done in agricultural goods, whose prices could change during the day, and hear of tough competition for certain jobs and lack of contenders for others. Clearly, there is a lot of explanatory work to be done to 'reconciliate' these findings with our previous model. But it is important to realize that the differences between model and reality should not be interpreted as a measure of the failure of the Soviet leaders to create the allocation system they wanted. Their ideal economic system, as stated above, is simply not known to us.

The Soviet Economic System and the Model of Completely Centralized Allocation

In the CC model the problem of co-ordinating all allocation decisions in the CMA was no problem: the CMA was assumed to dispose of perfect information and to rely on each household member – as consumer and producer – to act in the spirit of the CMA; 'consistent allocation decisions were easily formulated by the CMA and carried out to the last letter'. In terms of institutional characteristics, the CMA of the CC model could be imagined to be a giant computer centre, which at any time *immediately* absorbs any new information and translates it into consistent allocation decisions.

The Problem of Co-ordination
In real life, the enormity of the co-ordination (or information) problem has made it impossible to achieve such instantaneous solutions of the allocation problem. Think of millions of household members jotting down their preferences with respect to consumption (food, housing and other amenities) and work (profession, place and wage) on long lists for the CMA to study and follow; and think of all the necessary inputs (raw materials, fuels, semi-fabricates, component parts, machinery etc.) in tens of thousands of enterprises and of the outputs necessary of other enterprises to deliver these inputs, and add up all the allocation decisions that must be made to carry this out – preferably in a consistent way! Clearly, it

must take a long *time* and much effort to collect and rework all the information necessary for a centralized solution of the allocation problem.

To solve the problem of co-ordination in a world without 'instantaneous solution computers' the CMA has had to organize the activity of *planning*. Planning may be defined as 'a process of preparing decisions for action in the future'. Because of the time it takes to collect and rework information, planning must start long before the beginning of the action period, which may be a year or so, depending on the context.

To economize on time and resources the CMA has organized itself and the enterprises into a hierarchy of planning bodies, which specialize in planning at different levels of detail. In this way the CMA gets a better overview than if all planning had been done at the same level of detail and in one stroke. To what extent this CMA process of planning through a hierarchy means a decentralization of decision-making relative to the order suggested in the centralized model is hard to say and will not be further discussed. In the model it was simply assumed – with little specification as to how this was done – that all decisions were made in the CMA. In real life this is still roughly true. What has happened, however, with the introduction of information costs (and a non-perfect consensus of values) is that the allocation process in the CMA has become so much more complicated and rich in institutions and characteristic problems than the model CMA that it deserves a description in its own right. We now turn to this description, beginning with the hierarchy and ending with the process of planning. Before this a short comment and a delimitation of the field of study are in place.

First, all CMA allocation decisions are not made in Moscow. In reality, the all-union CMA is split up into state sub-CMAs to make the planning problem more manageable. These sub-CMAs – in state capitals – will in turn delegate part of their responsibilities to yet lower regional bodies, according to whether the production and consumption of a good is of local significance, for example. We shall not have room to pursue this regional aspect of planning at any length.

Second, to avoid unnecessary detail the following exposition will concentrate on the fairly uniform principles of allocation that apply within the dominating sector of the Soviet economy known as mining and manufacturing, in the following also referred to simply as 'the industrial sector'. This means that agriculture, trade and transport will not be dealt with specifically. It should also be noted that the allocation or planning schedule described below relates to the period before the celebrated 'industrial associations' reforms of 1973, the outcome of which is still largely unknown.

Soviet mining and manufacturing – a giant industry group. It is instructive for the Western student of the Soviet economic system to conceive of this as a giant group of companies of the type prevalent in the United States and Western Europe (e.g. General Motors, Unilever).

The board of directors (or possibly the stockholders) of the industry group would correspond to the government and party leadership (Politburo) in the Soviet Union. The executive board and the managing director heading it would have as their approximate opposite numbers the State Planning Committee, Gosplan, and its chairman. The various product lines and the corresponding divisions of the Western group would have their Soviet counterpart in the industries within mining and manufacturing and the ministries administering them. Special sub-divisions of the Western group for separate products or regions etc. would correspond to the main administration of the ministries (the so-called *glavki*) or to regional associations of enterprises (*obedinenije*) in the Soviet economy. The factories of the Western group, finally, would have their natural counterpart in Soviet producing enterprises. Both the Western and the Soviet group are organized in hierarchies and allocation decisions may be highly centralized.

However, the parallel should not be stretched too far. First, the Western industry group is typically engaged in only a limited number of product lines, whereas the Soviet group is infinitely much more versatile and complex; indeed, it comprises the whole set of activities within mining and manufacturing. With all its tens of thousands of enterprises the Soviet group is incomparably bigger than the typical Western group and so the problems of information and co-ordination are much greater in the Soviet case.

Second, the Soviet group finds itself dispersed in a federation, consisting of fifteen member states (republics) and a great number of administrative regions within them. All these have their special interests to look after as decisions are made in Moscow. In addition, most of these republics and regions are populated by peoples of different nationalities; history and tradition differ strongly between many of them and the level of education also varies in different parts of the Soviet Union. Such factors could work out negatively on the general consensus of values within the Soviet society. The smaller the frame of reference that people have in common, the more likely it becomes that central policies and instructions will be misunderstood or misinterpreted. The message will be deformed and the decisions executed will diverge from those planned for by the CMA. The typical Western group would have a more homogeneous environment to work in.

It should be added, however, as a third point, that in most cases the Western group forms only part of an industry or market. As a consequence, it must constantly pay attention to the behaviour of foreign as well as domestic competitors. In contrast, the Soviet group comprises by and large all enterprises in all industries. Competition between domestic enterprises is very weak and there is no foreign competition to speak of. This might instead facilitate planning in the Soviet case.

Production Planning in the Soviet Economy

The instrument, then, of centralized co-ordination of allocation decisions in the industrial sector is the plan. Basically, there are two types of plans, five-year plans (long-term) and annual plans (short-term). The best-known of these is probably the five-year plan, which gives an overall view of the main directions of economic development during the five years following its publication (e.g. the planned rate of increase of industrial production, the planned distribution of investments with respect to various industries, etc.). The five-year plan could be characterized as a combination of an action programme and a list of wishes; it does not contain direct decisions on production.

The annual plan is based on the long-term guidelines of the five-year plan. It is an operational plan which aims at providing the enterprises with detailed directives concerning what should be produced and how this should be done. In the following the interest will be focused on this chief document of co-ordination.

The planning hierarchy. The Soviet mining and manufacturing is administered according to what may be called *the industry principle.* Instead of making regional authorities all over the country responsible for the administration of all the enterprises within their respective regions, enterprises have been divided into industries and correspondingly subordinated to specialized *ministries*. These central ministries, for example, those of the metal-working industry, the electronics industry and the chemical industry, are responsible for the administration of the whole of an industry.

Operatively, the ministries are subdivided into *main administrations* or *glavki* (from *glavnaja kommissija* – main committee). They are responsible for the administration of specific products (coal, oil, etc.) or product groups within their respective ministry. To cite an example, the ministry for the machine building industry most likely has a *glavk* to administer the production of cars and another to run the shipbuilding activities of the industry.

In most cases the main administrations plan the operations of the producing enterprises. However, since the beginning of the 1960s this has increasingly become the task of the new *industrial associations*. These associations, which are a new link in the planning hierarchy (replacing largely the old *glavki*), are formed of a limited number of relatively small enterprises, which produce similar products or provide some other basis for a common administration. Typical instances of industrial associations would be those of the foodstuffs or textile industries, formed on a regional basis.

At the bottom of the hierarchy we find *the producing enterprises*. Depending upon their size, strategic importance and a number of other factors, these are subordinated to industrial associations or main administrations, or, in rare cases, even to ministries directly.

The planning process.   It is the purpose of the planning process to produce a set of instructions (or a plan) for the producing enterprises during the *plan* year. This plan should be ready *before* the plan year starts, i.e. towards the end of the *planning* year. The enormity of the co-ordination problem makes it necessary to start the planning process quite early in the planning year; the magnitude of the task is perhaps better understood if it is added that the plan not only should contain instructions as to what should be produced and how, but also should specify where all deliveries should come from and go to.

So the first step in the planning process is taken in the spring months of the planning year, when the government, assisted by Gosplan, decides on a set of preliminary, main guidelines for national economic development in the plan year, say 1977. These guidelines will suggest the planned rate of increase of the national

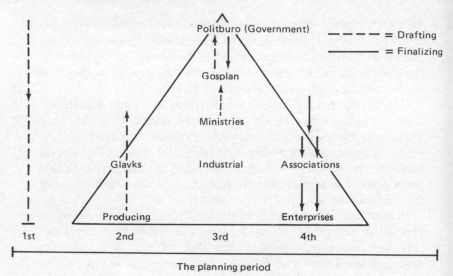

Figure 3.1 The planning stages

income, the proportions of it going to consumption and investment, the rate of increase of labour productivity and of production, which may be specified in the case of a few very important goods (e.g. steel, oil), the development of foreign trade, etc. These global-type judgements are based partly on the actual economic results of the previous year (in this case, 1975), partly on the preliminary economic record of the first quarter (and half) of the planning year (1976), partly on the estimated development of the economy during the second half of the planning year, and partly also on the general policies of the current five-year plan. The guidelines are then sent downwards through all the layers of the planning hierarchy.

It is now that the planning process really gets off to a start. Examining the central guidelines in the light of their own expectations and judgements, the various ministries now begin to work out draft targets for their production areas. However, such drafting activities go on also in the *glavki*, in the industrial associations and, not least, in the producing enterprises themselves – in increasing degree of detail.

It is valuable for the ministry-level planners to get the independent judgements of the enterprises on their production possibilities in this way. But there is no guarantee that the draft targets suggested by them will add up in such a way that they are in agreement with the ministry's draft targets. Neither can it be taken for granted that the individual ministries' draft targets are consistent with each other.

The second stage in the planning process is therefore to add up the draft output targets of the enterprises (and industrial associations) at *glavk* or ministry level to see how they compare with the preliminary ministry targets. If it appears now that the sum of the enterprises' targets falls short of the ministry target, then the ministry planners must do something about this. Most often they will try to talk enterprise managers into higher targets, but sometimes they may also reconsider the ministry target and lower it.

Once a unified set of draft targets has been arrived at with respect to the ministry's outputs, it must be studied if the output targets of all the individual ministries are mutually consistent, i.e. if the outputs of ministry A, which also serve as inputs in the production of ministry B, are targeted in such volumes that ministry B can reach its draft output targets.

Gosplan, the top planning body of the CMA, has a key role in this *overall consistency checkup*. It is to Gosplan that the ministries report about their unified draft output targets *and* the input supplies deemed necessary to achieve them. This reporting takes place around August–September of the planning year. In this third step of the planning process, the Gosplan thus checks the draft plans of the ministries to see if they are mutually consistent; also, it checks that the draft plans within mining and manufacturing are in line with the central guidelines. Each ministry has special departments to administer all outgoing (output) and ingoing (input) deliveries. These departments communicate directly with corresponding central, summary allocation departments in Gosplan. These summary departments work with so-called *material balances*, which are simply summary statements of the targeted needs and supplies of individual goods (like steel, wood, oil, etc.). Thousands of goods are interconnected through a vast network of such balances. The ultimate aim of the Gosplan planners is, of course, to see to it that all material balances are balanced, i.e. that the overall plan is consistent. Failing consistency in the material balances, in particular when targeted needs are in excess of supplies, Gosplan will first urge individual 'trouble ministries' to help close critical inconsistencies so that costly replanning on a large scale can be avoided. Should such actions not be successful, replanning may have to be made with several rounds of reiterations to ensure a consistent set of material balances. For instance, if the sum of targeted supplies of steel falls short of the targeted needs of steel for car production and ship construction, the car and ship production targets may have to be revised, which will in turn necessitate a number of consequential plan changes. Many of these changes will cause problems for the ministries – and enterprises! – involved, in the sense that they will be forced into target commitments that put them under strain. But Gosplan will not always 'win' such disputes. Instead, the usual procedure would seem to be that negotiations are taken up – in the form of an intensive exchange of information – to find a solution that is mutually acceptable. From October and some time onwards lively discussions of this kind are held in Moscow. These negotiations have certain similarities with the wage negotiations in the market economies.

When, as a result of its material balancing, reiterations and negotiations, Gosplan has produced what seems to be a consistent national economic plan with respect to all important inputs and outputs, the plan is sent to the government (and the party) for approval.

When the government has accepted the Gosplan proposal the planning process moves into its fourth, laborious stage. The set of overall targets must now be broken down in such detail that the individual enterprise can get the necessary operational instructions to fulfil or implement the plan. When the CMA planners set about to formulate a plan in such a way that they can be reasonably sure that it will actually be implemented they will face a number of complications.

They will soon find that, however big the number of goods entered into Gosplan's consistency plan, they will not by far cover all the needed inputs in mining and manufacturing. While some of these inputs, like sand or concrete, might be provided locally, other input deliveries may have to be planned on a more regular basis between ministries. In this sense, going from overall 'Gosplan consistency' to detail consistency means a great deal of additional planning effort below the Gosplan level.

Specifying the so-called *techpromfinplan* (technical, industrial, financial plan) of all enterprises – how much of semi-fabricate X should be used to produce good Y in enterprise Z, etc. – is laborious enough as it is. To complicate matters even more, there might have emerged a number of enterprises that, through the high requirements placed on them in the name of consistency, would be reluctant to accept the (low) input–output norms that the CMA planners might want to place on them; in such cases, planners would have to look closer into the problem of how managers could be motivated into particular commitments so that the plan does not fail.

This concludes our description of the planning process proper, in the sense of what new information must be collected each planning year and moved up and down the planning hierarchy. It should be added only that formally the final version of the plan goes to the legislative assembly, the Supreme Soviet, in December for approval, whereby it is given the nature of a law, binding – on certain conditions – to all agents of planning and production.

Problems in Planning – Three Interesting Aspects
However, there are many additional aspects on the problem of formulating an 'implementable' plan. One, to which we now turn, has to do with how planners could handle uncertainty, when the plan is laid down in detail.

Interval instructions v. point instructions. In real life, it has already been asserted, the CMA planners do not have perfect information about the production possibilities of the enterprises; neither can they be sure that what information they have is not systematically distorted – the managers' consensus of values may not be perfect. One way of interpreting this lack of perfect, truthful information in the CMA planning office is to say that there is *uncertainty* in the plan. This uncertainty is greatly expanded if it is taken into consideration that the CMA planners *cannot* predict all that is going to happen in the plan year, i.e. once actual production has started.

To take such cases of uncertainty or imperfection into account the CMA planners must supplement the enterprise plan with types of instructions *other* than simple *point* instructions like 'produce so much of A using so much of B and C!' Of course, in cases where production technology is long since established and input–output coefficients well-known, such point instructions might work. But in other cases where it is less well-known it would be more practical to work with an *interval* instruction, i.e. to allow the enterprise to use a little more – or a little less! – of a certain input (say fuel) to produce a given output.

Now if several enterprises were equipped with an interval instruction for one and the same good it might be hoped that positive and negative surprises in actual production for all the relevant enterprises would even out, so that 'on an average' actual input needs could come close to planned input needs. The problem is, however, that even in this fortunate situation it would still be necessary to transfer resources from enterprises with excess inputs to those with deficit inputs. Therefore the CMA planners have tried to direct the enterprises' use of inputs more precisely to *one* preferred point in the interval, i.e. to one certain input–output coefficient such that, if it is reached, this will mean a minimum of extra complications for the CMA planners. The technique used is to relate the reaching of the preferred point – and all other points in the interval – to a set of potential rewards or bonuses. This type of reward-related plan instruction is often referred to as a (plan) indicator (*pokazatel*).

A host of considerations will affect the choice of a 'reward function'. For instance, if it is believed by the planners that a certain input good will be in very short supply in the plan period, they may assign a fairly high reward to attaining the input–output norm with respect to this particular good. Again, if it is believed that the cost – in terms of complications for the planning process – of forgoing a unit of a certain output good is high the planners may suggest an equally large difference in reward between reaching and missing – by one unit! – the preferred point. This kind of reasoning applies with special strength if a loss of output would even make replanning necessary. This type of situation is really the one that the *pokazateli* are designed to avoid: they should – in the event of unforeseen disturbances in production – help the enterprise hold on to the original plan: the *pokazateli* are really a kind of *adjustment* instructions.

Which plan variables should then be selected for interval instructions and which for point instructions? This issue we can only comment on briefly here. It has been suggested above that the simpler and the better-known the production technology, the more likely it is that the CMA will choose point instructions when input–output norms are laid down in the plan. An input of a specific nature is labour, the supply of which may be scarce (and uncertain) and so suggest the use of an additional labour input indicator – e.g. in the form of the wage sum – to make it costly to the enterprise to use 'too much' labour: a similar reasoning could, of course, be applied to the input of (investment) capital in production.

On the output side CMA planners can also use interval instructions or indicators to direct enterprises to certain preferred 'solutions'. For instance, if the output of a good X is considered to be especially important and/or uncertain it may be practical to tie a bonus of some sort to plan fulfilment.

In the foregoing paragraphs planning has been discussed almost exclusively in physical terms. In the CC model also, there was no need for money and prices to enter into central decision-making. In real life, however, there may arise planning problems that are more easily solved with prices (and money) than without. Take, for instance, the case of a clothing enterprise which produces a wide range of clothes to satisfy seasonally changing needs. The planners above the enterprise level will not be interested in the detail *composition* of output, only that the *volume* of output for a given input is as large as possible. To be able to add shirts and trousers, however, the planners must reduce them to a common measuring rod, which is prices. Ideally, these prices should reflect the relative scarcities of shirts and trousers – like the prices of the CD model. But in these sections of the CMA-planned economy there are no markets in the CD model sense and, as a consequence, no such *scarcity* prices. Theoretically, one might conceive of the CMA working out such 'shadow' prices internally. In actual practice, however, the prices worked with are simple *cost-plus prices* – based on the average unit production cost in all enterprises producing a good – that tend to be changed fairly seldom. While such *accounting* prices are no perfect basis for 'decentralizing' decisions on the detail composition of output, they may still serve this purpose better than if these decisions were made above the enterprise level.

Through prices it will be possible to provide the enterprise with an output instruction – of the point or interval type – that, say, 3 million roubles' worth of clothing be produced by enterprise Z, the detail composition of which the enterprise may determine itself. In principle, one might have thought the same approach could be used on the input side, the instruction then being that the enterprise should produce a certain output volume through inputs not exceeding, say 2.5 million roubles' worth. But the enterprise's choice of inputs may not be consistent with the deliveries planned to go to other enterprises and so could threaten the plan. Therefore value-term instructions (instead of physical) cannot really be applied in central planning on the input side – or, for that matter, on the output side, when the output is an intermediate good and does not (like textiles) go directly to final consumption. This, however, does not preclude the use of value-term instructions with respect to employment or variable capital to incite good economy in the enterprise – *given* a consistent set of inputs and outputs. Neither, indeed, is it precluded that the CMA calculates a value-term measure, where from the sum of CMA-priced and CMA-planned outputs is deducted the sum of CMA-priced and CMA-planned inputs, to yield 'profits', which is then presented to the enterprise like any other plan instruction. Such profit instructions were emphasized in the so-called economic reforms of 1965. The message conveyed through such an instruction from the CMA is that when the enterprise seeks to reduce costs or is thrown off its plan, it should choose such measures that the net addition to this 'profits' measure is as big as possible. The message is certainly *not*, as seems to have been believed by some observers of the Soviet scene, that Soviet enterprises have become 'profit-maximizers' in the sense that the market economy enterprise is thought to behave. Any such similarity is wholly out of place, since the Soviet enterprise still typically has its planned inputs and outputs determined centrally, and not through the market.

While the economic reforms must not be interpreted to have led to any significant increase in the importance of market allocation in the Soviet Union, it was in their spirit to redistribute minor allocation decisions to lower levels in the planning hierarchy. This was attempted by eliminating a great number of physical term indicators, which had become so many that the bonus effects of allocation decisions were hardly visible to either planner or to manager. In other cases, the bonus effects of a certain decision were only too visible – the examples abound. For instance, a textile-producing enterprise has got a plan from the CMA. The gross production indicator for a certain quality A appears to be the most important indicator – in terms of bonus opportunities upon plan fulfilment. The indicator is expressed in running yards. By narrowing the width of the cloth the manager can easily fulfil the plan and reap his bonus without any formal mistake.

Examples like this one should probably not be regarded as the typical case. But they point to a general problem of designing plan instructions: in their effort to direct the manager to a certain achievement – e.g. saving on a specific input – CMA planners tend to overlook other important aspects of production.

One way to avoid such over-emphasis on certain activities would be to use more of value-term instructions. This would give the enterprise management itself greater leeway to choose the proper output combination – independently of any preconceived bias of the planner. This is where the profit indicator comes into the picture. However, as was just said, the requirement by the CMA planners that there be a consistent set of planned input deliveries puts a rather strict limitation on the use of value-term instructions, in particular on the input side. For then there must be a ready set of delivery contracts between all enterprises when the plan period starts.

This brings us over to another aspect of the problem of formulating an 'implementable' plan, that of contracting.

Delivery contracts under centralized allocation. The mere knowledge that in some office in Gosplan there is – on paper – a consistent set of material balances will not, by experience, be sufficient for the managers as a guarantee that all the necessary inputs will actually be delivered. In addition, they will want to con-clude formal contracts about planned deliveries between enterprises. Such contracts will perform many useful functions: the enterprise scheduled to deliver will have qualities, quantities and dates specified; the enterprise scheduled to receive will have a standard against which it can compare actual delivery performance; and, not least, in the event of unforeseen problems of delivery any higher authority will have a legal instrument to judge by.

The need for contracting stems from the fact that it has not been possible (or desirable) for the planners to feed so much information into the plan that all enterprise managers can take plan fulfilment for certain. Also, in the case of mishaps individual managers cannot rely on other managers or ministers competing for the deficit goods to act 'justly', for in such matters there may not be a consensus of values between them. In the CD model it was emphasized that 'a common set of [transaction] rules' was crucial in promoting market exchange. In the centralized economy, too – though different in content – contracts are important to help in plan implementation.

The plan in action – the need for warning signals and adjustments. However carefully indicators and contracts have been specified, once the plan goes into action things are bound to happen that were not foreseen, like production disturbances, etc. They impose new tasks on planners – and managers. For the planners it becomes vital to know in time if and where production has run into problems, so that counter-measures can be taken before any costly replanning becomes necessary. To this end various warning signals have been instituted by the CMA: one is the so-called 'control by the rouble' (*kontrol rublem*) which is simply the reporting by the state (monopoly) bank of enterprise plan fulfilment or not; another check-up is carried out by party representatives in the enterprise.

But the planners above enterprise level will not intervene if it is not absolutely necessary. If the managers can solve the problem of deficit inputs through mishaps with *planned* deliveries by providing *unplanned* deliveries through actions of their own, the planners will not object. In fact, there is a not-unimportant, unofficial sideline activity in many Soviet enterprises by so-called fixers (*tolkachi*), whose job it is to buy and sell goods in deficit or excess of the plan to help the enterprise win potential bonuses. The fixers could be said to operate in what looks like markets between enterprises. These markets, though, are very remote from those of the CD model: they are unofficial, temporary and narrow and prices are typically renegotiated, i.e. affected by individual buyers and sellers, in every new transaction.

These outside-plan activities help the enterprises stay inside the plan, which is desirable. But they have an undesirable property, too, in that the CMA planners will not get the necessary *feedback* information about what went wrong with the plan, if all non-fulfilment is 'saved' by extraneous actions. This, however, is a price CMA planners will often gladly pay to be relieved of the need for permanent interventions for adjustment.

Production Planning: The Case of Labour
In the foregoing section the problem of production planning was discussed with no emphasis on any specific input or output. In this section we will focus attention on the allocation of labour. Again, we begin by returning to the CC model.

In the CC model allocating jobs to workers was no problem. The CMA disposed of perfect information both as to all jobs available and as to all workers eligible. In the event of any inconsistency, the CMA planners could always count on the perfect consensus of values of the workers to help them: there would always be a worker willing to follow the instructions of the CMA and take the job that would close the inconsistency.

In the real world it has not been possible to operate the system in this way. It has not been viable for the CMA to assign a specific job to each individual worker because of the overwhelming costs of information this would imply. Also, the consensus of values of the workers with the planners does not seem to have been sufficient to guarantee that any such assignment would actually work in practice. Instead, the CMA has had to rely on a system of labour allocation, in which the working household members may choose at will among the jobs offered by the CMA. This, clearly, means a good deal more decentralization than in the CC model. Indeed, the CMA could be said to use markets to allocate labour. But then it must be emphasized that these markets have certain properties that modify the nature of decentralization. We now turn to these properties.

First, the principal right to choose a job at will is subject to some specific limitations. For instance, the CMA may direct certain categories of people to specific jobs. This is reportedly the case with university students during the first three years after graduation.

Second, when the remaining, 'non-directed' workers are free to choose jobs among those offered it is important to remember that it is the CMA that decides what jobs should be offered. On the basis of what consumption goods and other goods the CMA has decided to produce, a plan must be drawn up well before actual production. This plan must also describe all the jobs that must be taken care of to have the plan carried out. Thus, at least for a one-year period, it is a rather *fixed* set of jobs that the working household members may choose among. In the decentralized model economy, if at the going market-determined wages some enterprises or industries could not go along with their production programme for lack of labour then these programmes would have to be *recast* and a new set of jobs would be offered in the labour markets; as a corollary the wage structure would change. In the Soviet allocation system, obviously, there is much less of this kind of automatic adjustment of production in response to situations of, say, deficit supply of labour in various lines of production. Of course, it will be wise for the CMA to take the existing pattern of available workers into due consideration when production is planned in the first place. But when deficit – or surplus – situations with respect to labour arise in actual production the CMA will be reluctant to change the global production plan in operation. Instead it will appeal to the workers to choose an occupation that corresponds with the production plan. Another way of expressing this is to say that in the Soviet allocation system, when the jobs offered through the CMA are not consistent with the jobs desired by the workers, a relatively large part of the burden of adjustment will be borne by the workers in the sense that many simply will not get the desired jobs! This is an important qualification when we speak of the (partly) decentralized allocation of labour in the Soviet Union.

A third, connected property of the labour market is that the CMA determines the structure and level of *wages* as well. There are no negotiations of wages on the pattern of those in, say, the Western European market economies. This does not mean that the CMA is wholly free to fix wages. For instance, if there is a recurring shortage of labour in certain geographical or occupational areas and little return to pure appeals, the CMA will have to increase wages there to induce workers to go there. But then, of course, there may be several different wage structures that can secure consistency in labour allocation in the planners' sense of getting all jobs manned. Which specific wage structure will be preferred by the CMA will depend on a host of additional considerations that policy planners may want to make, i.e. rewarding heavy and dirty jobs, stimulating interest in research and teaching jobs in a more long-run perspective, etc.

To what extent – fourth – the CMA will have to adjust the wage structure to achieve consistency in the allocation of labour will depend also on the general conditions under which the CMA offers jobs to the public. Most important here is the *information* available to workers on alternative job opportunities through, say, labour exchanges; it would seem that in the Soviet Union little such information is made available by the state (monopoly) employer, which is also in a position to select only such information as would help the CMA to secure consistency. Equally important is the existence of *unemployment insurance* and related legislation; it would seem that in the Soviet Union there is no state unemployment insurance; also, a person who has been voluntarily unemployed for six months will then become subject to laws that will make it quite problematic for him or her to continue to be without a job. A third aspect is that of the situation in *housing*; if the supply of housing is tight in wide areas, and rationed through the employer as well, then this will work out negatively on labour mobility – and, indeed, imply a lesser degree of decentralization of labour allocation than otherwise.

In sum: information costs, etc., have made it impossible to allocate labour according to the completely centralized model. Instead the CMA has had to rely on an allocation system that resembles a decentralized market. At given wages workers choose their jobs freely. On closer inspection, however, it appears that there are very definite limits to the decentralization: the CMA controls both the supply of jobs and the wages and is not very generous to those who do not comply. Still it may be reasonable to speak of some decentralization in the allocation of labour.

Allocating Consumer Goods: A Set of Markets in the Centralized Economy

Above, production planning was discussed with little specific reference to whether the goods concerned were intended for further use in production or were consumer goods. We must now look closer into the latter category, i.e. consumer goods, and discuss both the production planning and, in particular, the allocation of such goods to the households. For here there are some interesting differences between the CC model and Soviet reality.

The fundamental observation to be made, again, is that in the Soviet economy decisions on how much resources should go to the production of consumer goods and how much should be produced of important consumer goods are made centrally. But the actual solution of this problem is very different from the CD model solution, where the individual household members had their preferences effected through the CMA directly into their hands.

To economize on information costs, the CMA has had to resort to simpler methods to determine what consumer goods should be produced in what quantities. Basing the consumption plan for, say, next year on last year's production and/or actual consumption of such goods, the CMA could get suggestive evidence on possible development patterns either through sample studies at home or through studying consumption in other countries at relevant income levels. Another source of information that comes to mind are the queues (so well-known to foreign visitors), the idea being that where there is a queue there is excess demand. One problem is that it is not always obvious whether this excess demand refers to the actual good or to the personnel situation in the shops!

If planning the supply of consumer goods in this way is different in technique from that of the CC model, the degree of centralization of decision-making is the same. How, then, should these goods be allocated to the households? Since the CMA does not know the desires of the individual households, there would be little point in allocating specific bundles of consumer goods directly to each household. Instead the CMA divides the totality of consumer goods into big 'blocks', which are then distributed by geographical regions and then offered to the general public through retail shops run by the state. In the completely centralized model these goods were allocated directly to the individual households and so there was no need for money and prices. But would it work to let people come into the shops and make their choices among goods that were offered free of charge? While this might work theoretically in a world where people were perfectly honest and planners perfectly lucky, the CMA has preferred not to rely on this small chance. Instead the CMA has put prices on the goods to help allocate them. With this we have come to the apparent similarity between the situations faced by American and Soviet households alike: the consumer himself decides what to buy on the basis of given prices. This is an important element of decentralization of allocation decisions in the Soviet economy.

It is tempting – and in a sense correct – to say that the centralized Soviet economy makes use of markets to allocate consumer goods. But it is vital to recognize that this market arrangement is fundamentally different from the market system of the decentralized market economy. In the latter system the total production volumes and the prices of goods in individual markets cannot be even predicted by the CMA or anyone else. In the Soviet economy, in contrast, the CMA can determine both volume and price within wide limits; also, in the market system an increase in the relative price of a good should be expected to call forward extra supplies on to the market, whereas this would not necessarily hold in the Soviet economy.

Now on what criterion – or criteria – should the CMA price the goods offered to the households in quantities determined by itself? Of course, there are certain limits to what prices can be chosen; e.g., the price must not be fixed so high that the quantity demanded is smaller than the quantity supplied, for then inventories will pile up and inconsistency be the result. Likewise, if the CMA chooses to set a price that is so low that at this price quantity demanded is bigger than the quantity supplied – i.e. a situation of excess demand – this is also an inconsistency in the sense that all that is demanded cannot be sold or carried over to the households; the greater the excess demand for a good, though, the more likely it is that the 'pure' allocation through the market will be supplemented by other allocative measures either by the CMA or by the households themselves.

The criteria introduced in pricing will typically have to do with social goals on the part of the CMA. If policy planners think it desirable to hold down the consumption of things like alcoholic drinks and furs, they will – in addition to determining a moderate volume of production – set the prices high (i.e. relative to the costs of production). Conversely, if they want to induce people to certain kinds of consumption they will set the prices low; instances of this would be books and other objects of cultural consumption.

Considerations of income distribution, or more broadly of what should be the basic components of family welfare, dictate price policy in other fields. Take for instance children's clothing, which is priced quite low in the Soviet economy, or rents, which are very low, or medical care services, which are free of charge. In the case of housing rents have been set so low that it has not been possible to allocate dwellings solely through the market. Lots of households are queuing to get another apartment and the CMA has had to set up an organization to determine who should get what. Similarly, in the case of medical services the market must be assisted by state administration to match the limited resources with the unlimited needs. This is the case, where we are back in the model of centralized resource allocation again.

In a number of consumer capital goods markets, like those for cars and colour television sets, there is also a long-standing situation of excess demand. Here the reason is not that the CMA has set the price lower than the cost of production – in fact, it is very likely at or above this cost – but that it has determined that the volume of production should not be any larger. In many cases, of course, where the costs of production are unknown it is impossible to say what extent the excess demand derives from the price or the quantity decision. In general, however, the often-observed situations of excess demand in the Soviet consumer goods markets may have a logical explanation in centralized allocation system itself. It is that in the choice between unexpected excess demand and excess supply in the market the CMA planners will prefer the former: for while some of the consumers will then return empty-handed from the shops, all goods will be sold and the planners can concentrate on planning for an increase in the coming plan; with excess supply planners will have a problem to dispose of the goods and, even worse, to plan production for the next period ('the supply-constrained economy').

Excess demand markets may cause problems when the shortage is much felt by the households and no special rationing method other than price has been introduced by the CMA. It may then pay some people to buy goods in the public market only to resell them at a higher price for private profit to other people who have money but do not want to wait their turn with everybody else. Such so-called 'black market' activity is prohibited by law with very severe penalties, but there is reason to believe that it still occurs to a non-negligible extent in the Soviet economy today.

It should be obvious from this discussion of how the CMA exchanges consumer goods through markets that, for all the decentralization of *buyers'* decisions it means, this allocation method differs in many important respects from that of the decentralized market economy. Most important, there is no corresponding decentralization on the sellers' side or with respect to price.

'True' decentralization in the kolkhoz *markets.* Mention should also be made of an area in the Soviet economy that has come to function outside the CMA domain, and so must work by decentralization.

In the so-called free *kolkhoz* (collective farm) markets, the decisions about what and how much should be produced are decentralized and prices formed in the market. The supply in these markets come from the private plots of both *kolkhoz* and *sovchoz* (state farm) workers and from joint *kolkhoz* production in excess of centrally decided deliveries to the state. The *kolkhoz* markets are an important contributor of foodstuffs to the cities.

Prices form quite freely in these markets, without any intervention by the CMA. Households and 'enterprises' observe the changes in the freely fluctuating market price as they make their decisions about what to buy and sell. It seems likely that the part-time working 'entrepreneurs' should in general regard the market price as given and impossible to affect through measures of their own.

It is true that the prices that actually come about in these markets are also influenced by the decisions of the CMA in neighbouring fields such as those of agricultural production in general (the CMA decides on prices and quantities available of the machines, fuel, etc. that the farms buy off the state) and the consumption of foodstuffs, which are sold through a large number of state retail outlets, run by the CMA. However, in this context we have chosen largely to leave out these aspects. From the point of view of resource allocation the interesting feature of these markets is that here households *and* entrepreneurs react ɔn price changes that are *not* directly regulated by the CMA.

Decentralization of consumer goods allocation – its relative importance. It is hard to find a reliable measure that summarizes the importance of consumer goods allocation through decentralization i.e. through CMA-controlled or *kolkhoz* markets – relative to consumption as a whole. The reasons have to do with problems of statistical coverage and definitions and, not least, with how CMA-determined prices should be interpreted and used for purposes of addition. In this short book there is not room for a discussion of these problems, however, and so we simply try to provide a roundabout measure.

This measure computed from official Soviet sources is based on two statistics: (1) the value of state and co-operative retail sales plus the value of *kolkhoz* market sales net of indirect taxes and (2) the value of goods and services allocated directly by the CMA (health and medical services, education and research, defence, administration, etc.). If these two statistics are added and (1) set in relation to the sum, the proportion turns out to be around two-thirds, i.e. 60–70 per cent of the resources used for consumption in the Soviet Union are allocated in ways that are *less* centralized than that prescribed by the CC model. This may surprise many students, but should *not* lead to the conclusion – for reasons cited above – that the Soviet economy is a market economy along the lines of the decentralized allocation model.

Summary

We chose to study the economic system of the Soviet Union because it has long been looked upon as a prototype of the centralized economy. How far the Soviet Union leaders have wanted to centralize economic decision-making is not known. The CC model has been used as a background or starting point mainly because of the insights it provides into the fundamentals of centralization.

Central co-ordination of economic decision-making is performed in the Soviet economy through planning. To cope with all the millions of allocation decisions that must be made, a planning hierarchy has been set up, which collects and reworks information at different levels and reiterates the eventual document of co-ordination – the plan – a number of times to achieve consistency;

this is the planning process, which must start long in advance of the production period to be finished in time.

Since collecting and reworking information is costly, it has been necessary to try to save on detail planning. This can be done by giving the enterprises interval instructions rather than point instructions in their operational plans. There are definite limits, however, as to how far such 'decentralization' may go.

Once it has been decided by the CMA how much should be produced of each good, consumer goods are allocated to the consumers via a market at centrally determined prices. This represents an element of decentralization relative to the CC model. But these markets are fundamentally different from those of the market economy. The closest approximation of the latter to be found in the Soviet Union are probably the so-called 'kolkhoz markets'.

3.3 RESOURCE ALLOCATION IN FRANCE

The French economic system is interesting above all on account of what by Western European standards is a pronounced element of central economic planning. Indeed, there are those who claim that the French have created a new type of planning. Others, however, have been more sceptical, feeling that the true significance of French planning has been overrated.

Whatever one's assessment of French planning, there can be no doubt that the French planning ideology has been shaped in an economic system that is different from that of the United States, even though the French system, too, is predominantly a decentralized one. In this section we shall consider the differences between these two systems and eventually also compare French planning with that of the Soviet Union.

Clearly, the French have long had an attitude to the state and to competition that is very much their own. This will probably also go a long way towards explaining their ideas concerning planning. Before going into the allocation system, we shall therefore take a quick look at the historical background.

A Sketch of the Background

France was a fully fledged nation-state already in the seventeenth century. Mercantilist thinking soon gave rise to a state with far-reaching economic powers. To a great extent it was the state that regulated both trade and the industrial sector and that determined the pattern of foreign trade – apart from its traditional spheres of activity (tax collection, etc.).

The French Revolution at the end of the eighteenth century gave birth to the new ideas of individual liberty that were manifested above all in the increasing power of the bourgeoisie throughout the nineteenth century. The new concept of liberty was similar to the American competitive ideology already described. Each individual should have the right to make the most for himself of his own capabilities. But the French 'doctrine of liberty' never acquired the same individualism in economic matters and the same hostility to the state as its American counterpart. The state in France had completely different traditions to build on; it seemed easier for the state to co-operate with commerce and industry. Nor did competition there become as fierce as in the United States. The 'survival of the fittest' mentality did not acquire anything like the same footing in France.

How, then, has the particular ideology of the French worked out on the economic system of France? In the following we try to answer briefly this question by comparing, first, the real-life French system with the real-life American system to see the differences in the degree of decentralization of decision-making; next we try to give a condensed judgement of some basic characteristics of state activity in France, this time in comparison with state activities both in the United States and the Soviet Union.

Degree of Decentralization

Consumption through the State

In France as in the United States, the households basically decide themselves how to use their incomes in the light of the information furnished by market prices. Market allocation is less important, however: for total household consumption (i.e. including public consumption) the proportion of goods and services that is allocated by state authorities is far greater in France than in the United States.

This difference is due to a number of factors. First, the social insurance system in France is far more advanced than in the United States. Second, medical services are produced and allocated through the state in France but not in the United States. Contributions in France are paid in the form of taxation by means of compulsory insurance. Third, practically all education in France is free and is run by the state, while in the United States this is true of primary and secondary education only. Like their American counterparts, the French households by and large decide for themselves how much of their labour they should offer in the market. The French labour market is characterized by a more comprehensive system of associations and wage negotiations, and so, in a sense, is less decentralized than the American labour market.

Less Competition and Less Concentration
Competition between enterprises in France is less intense than in the United States. Also, it has often been remarked in studies of the French economy that the French businessman does not have the same attitude to competition as his American colleagues. There seems to be a widespread feeling among French businessmen that competition should not be taken too far. Putting other enterprises out of business often seems to be regarded as a more or less immoral waste of the resources of the community. There is nothing to match the violent publicity and price wars that often break out between American enterprises. French enterprises will often aim at securing a particular share of the market or a particular status in a definite geographical region. Often they compete by means of quality rather than price. This picture of the competitive environment in which French enterprises operate is admittedly a simplification, but it will still serve as an indication of the differences existing between France and the United States in this field.

In France industries are typically much less concentrated than in the United States. France has very few counterparts of the gigantic American corporations discussed above, even though amalgamations and cartel formations have not in general been opposed by the state. In many cases the state actually encourages cartels, for instance where they are judged likely to result in social benefit through rationalization and specialization. Although the American type of anti-trust legislation also exists in France, it seems to be interpreted on very generous lines.

Some figures will show the difference: whereas the fifty largest enterprises in the United States in 1975 had a total sales value corresponding to almost 30 per cent of GNP, the same proportion in France was only just over 16 per cent. Comparing the 500 largest enterprises' share of GNP and of the number of gainfully employed persons, the American figures were 55 and 55 per cent respectively while the French figures were no more than 34 and 15 per cent respectively (1975).

In France too, however, we can also find a few industries where large enterprises of the American variety predominate. This is above all the case in the manufacturing industries: the motor industry, the electro-technical industry and the aluminium industry. Commerce and agriculture, on the other hand, are dominated by small units.

State Influence in the Business Sector

Among the very large enterprises not a few – e.g. the Renault motor manufacturing company – are owned by the state. Indeed, there are entire industries, e.g. the coal industry, oil and aircraft, where a majority of the enterprises are state-owned. Thus, although some 80 per cent of industrial output in France comes from enterprises in private hands, state-owned (or nationalized) enterprises are far more important in France than in the United States.

In is important to note, however, that state ownership does not necessarily mean that all economic decision-making is also centralized to the state. Typically these state companies operate 'on equal terms' in the market with other privately owned firms, and so do not imply any significant increase in the degree of centralization of decision-making.

However, there are some state-owned enterprises in France that are directly attached to the state budget and run under specific instructions, e.g. postal services and communications. Also, there is a more important group of state-owned enterprises which to all intents and purposes resemble the American public utilities (*societé nationale*); these include power stations and gas works, etc. Enterprises in this group are also quite closely dependent on central state authorities in the conduct of their business.

Thus, while state influence in the business sector is probably somewhat greater in France than in the United States, the difference should not be exaggerated. In France as in the United States, the majority of enterprises (even when they are state-owned) operate in markets and are guided in their decision-making by market prices, not by central state instructions.

Central Economic Planning in France

In the section on the Soviet Union it was described how comprehensive central planning was carried out by the CMA. The one-year plans contained fairly detailed orders to tens of thousands of enterprises about what should be produced, etc. Central economic planning in the Soviet Union was in fact instrumental to the entire functioning of the economy. Let us refer to Soviet planning as *direct central planning*.

A different situation applied in the United States. Here the majority of allocation decisions were taken independently by the micro-units, i.e. the households and enterprises. But the CMA was by no means insignificant. Many direct allocation decisions were taken at macro-level, so too were a host of decisions of economic policy having a more indirect bearing on resource allocation. Through fiscal and monetary policy the state was able to influence the economy as a whole – total employment, the level of prices and the balance of payments. In order to make decisions of this kind, the decision-making authorities must have a detailed knowledge of the workings of the economy. In this sense decisions of economic policy certainly call for some kind of central economic planning. But unlike central planning in the Soviet Union, American central planning does not result in any written public plan. The American type of planning could therefore be referred to instead as *indirect central planning*.

Indicative Central Planning

Central planning in France has been regarded by many as something midway between the Soviet and American types of planning. French central planning is often referred to as *indicative planning*.

In order to explain French central planning, we shall begin with a brief description of its more formal workings, i.e. of the bodies and institutions taking part in planning work. We shall then comment on the actual significance of French planning in the context of resource allocation.

The plan and the planning institutions. The French plan, like its Soviet counterpart, is a public document. But there, on the whole, the resemblance ends. In the first place, as we have already seen, French planning is not direct – like Soviet planning – but only indicative. It does not give the enterprises any direct instructions. Instead it rests content with informing them what actions would be desirable on their part in order for the manufacturing sector – and the economy as a whole – to attain certain fairly generally formulated goals. It should be emphasized that these goals are to a great extent the result of expert assessments within different industries, etc., so that we are not concerned here with politically determined goals of the kind that characterize Soviet plans.

Second, and this is really only another way of saying what has just been said, French planning is not nearly as detailed as Soviet planning. Plans are made for the level of industry, not for the enterprise level, and not even all branches of industry are represented, but only some 100–150.

Third, planning in France covers periods of five years and states goals for the terminal year only, not for the years leading up to it.

Fourth, there is a significant difference between French and Soviet planning as regards the number of people engaged in actual planning work. Soviet planning requires a gigantic administration with thousands of full-time officials at different levels. French planning work is done by a small staff of a few hundred persons. Here planning is based to a great extent on the participation of representatives of different trade organizations in the French economy (e.g. managers, farmers, trade unionists) together with government officials and academic experts. These people participate for various periods of time as experts in their special fields, generally without receiving any special remuneration in return.

What, then, is the object of French planning? To begin with (i.e. soon after the last war), specific production targets were set for certain sectors so that efforts could then be made to attain these targets with the aid of various kinds of state intervention. However, economic development and an increasing dependence on foreign trade have gradually changed the character of planning. The aim now is to give an overall picture of the future plans of different private sectors such as manufacturing and commerce, to check the consistency between such sectoral plans, and to relate them to more detailed plans for the development of the public sector.

Thus the most important task of the plan today seems to be to inform decision-makers in the business sector about a possible future development of the economy as a whole – and of the sectors – assuming that the plans of the individual sectors are actually put into practice. But the plan is also used as an instrument of regional development policy and as a means of co-ordinating activities between state and non-state enterprises in fields in which the state has particularly large interests, e.g. the steel industry and shipbuilding and engineering.

The importance of French planning. The actual effects of French indicative planning on resource allocation are hard to determine. Can France really be said, because of its central planning, to have a far more centralized economic system than the United States? Some people contend that planning in France implies a strong central direction of the economy. Others, and they are probably in the majority, credit French planning today with relatively little influence on resource allocation. The main value of the plan lies in the total picture of future economic development it provides. Nor should one neglect the intrinsic value of the actual publication of a national economic plan. This may facilitate a nation-wide effort for a rapid development of French society in both economic and other spheres.

Summary

The French economic system is somewhat similar to the American system, but there are important differences between them. Competition is generally less intense in France than in the United States, though the liberalization of trade and the Common Market have increased the degree of competitiveness in France. Also, consumption decisions are more centralized in France. The French public sector itself is larger than its American counterpart.

The importance of French central planning is a matter of dispute. There is no question of any centralization of allocation decisions on Soviet lines; for French central planning, which is often termed indicative, does not contain any direct orders to enterprises, only general guidelines and information concerning the economic development foreseen and desired by the state.

4. Economic Systems in a Broader Perspective

In chapters 2 and 3 of this book we have studied the mechanisms through which decisions concerning the allocation of scarce resources are made and co-ordinated in different economic systems. The basic way of characterizing different systems was to ask: are allocation decisions mainly centralized and co-ordinated through a state administrative apparatus, or are they mainly made independently by firms and households and co-ordinated through a system of markets and prices?

The economic system is, however, as pointed out already in the introductory chapter, only part of the complicated network of relations among people that characterizes any society. The economic system functions in a broader socio-political environment, and the rules and institutions that determine the economic system are continuously influenced more or less vigorously by various factors in this environment. The emphasis in this chapter will be on the interplay between the economic system and those factors of the socio-political environment that seem to have the most direct influence on the shaping of the economic system, such as the political system.

We will also consider the relationship between allocation system and structure of ownership and will then touch upon the old question whether a market economy is compatible with state (or 'socialist') ownership of the means of production.

Next, we take up the so-called convergence hypothesis for a

critical examination. This hypothesis or theory is a grand attempt to suggest a stable long-run relationship between the economic system and certain factors of the socio-political environment, in particular the level of development.

Finally, the development of the Yugoslav economic system since the Second World War is examined. The continuous social experimentation in this country – with changes both in the economic system and in the socio-political environment – makes it a good illustration of many of the points made earlier in the chapter.

4.1   THE SOCIO-POLITICAL ENVIRONMENT

What aspects of the socio-political environment are especially relevant to the analysis of economic systems? In figure 4.1 we have tried to distinguish some factors, the historical and ideological background, the size and geographical location, the level of development, the degree of openness and the political system. The list is by no means exhaustive. Also, it should be pointed out that some of the factors are strongly interdependent, like those of the size and geographical location and the degree of openness. Such interdependences will not be considered below, however, where the focus will be on the interplay between the economic system and the political system. But first we must deal briefly with the remaining factors of interest.

Ideology
That knowledge of the ideological and historical background is important for the understanding of economic systems we have already noted in the country studies in the United States, the Soviet Union and France. Americans, for instance, were said to be in favour of market allocation since they thought the rapid economic development experienced by the United States was in large part due to the market system. This seems to be a reasonable interpretation of American economic history. It should be added, though, that it was not the market system as such that did it. It was the market system *plus* several hundred years of time, in which people had learnt gradually how to organize production and business through markets. And markets, to be sure, did not arise out of nothing. Their

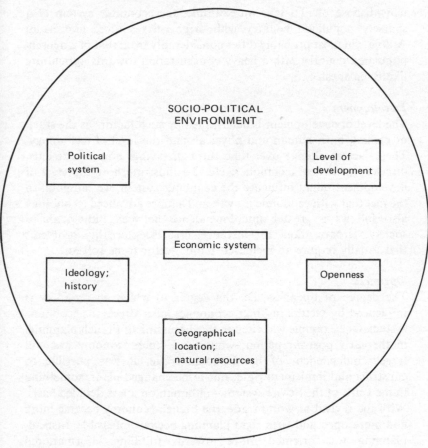

Figure 4.1 The socio-political environment

formation was much helped by the growth of nation-states, which could establish the necessary framework for market activity in terms of contract laws, courts, etc. Of course, when we look at economic ideologies in the present we cannot always go so deep down into economic history, but it is valuable to think sometimes of the long time it takes to shape consistent economic systems.

Geography
The size and geographical position determines the amount and kinds of natural resources (including climatic conditions) that an economy

may dispose of. To take an example, the economic system of a sparsely populated country with large oil resources like Saudi Arabia will most probably differ considerably from that of a densely populated country with a heavy concentration towards agriculture like Bangladesh.

Development

The level of development is determined by such factors as the stock of capital, both human and physical, and the level of technology. These factors change over time through savings and investments, discoveries of new techniques, etc. To illustrate how the level of development might influence the economic system, we can point to the fact that with economic growth and a more advanced technology also follows a greater interdependence between individuals in society. Urbanization, for instance, creates externality problems that usually require an increased public sector to be solved.

Openness

The degree of openness, i.e. the degree to which an economy is influenced by factors in *other* economies, also affects the economic system. One example was cited in the discussion of French planning: in the early postwar period, while the French economy was still largely independent of international trade, it was possible to construct and implement rigid, not-to-be-changed plans, something in the spirit of the Soviet system – although on a less detailed basis. With the revival of world trade, the French economy became more and more open and such rigid planning became infeasible. Instead, planning was oriented more towards fulfilling informational purposes, i.e. towards indicative planning. Similar types of problems are experienced in the small, trade-dependent economies of Eastern Europe, like Hungary and Czechoslovakia, when they expand their foreign trade, in particular with the market economies.

Resource Allocation and the Political System

In the above analysis of resource allocation in the United States, the Soviet Union and France it was found that, despite all the differences between them in terms of economic ideology and other aspects of the socio-political environment in the three countries, the state administrative apparatus – the CMA – had an important role to play in all three. The essence of this role is to co-ordinate economic activities – in the Soviet Union *instead* of markets, in the United States and France *in support* of markets – both through legislation and through current interventions in the system.

In the foregoing case studies we have described briefly how the CMA *works*. Little has been said, however, of how this working of the CMA can be *influenced* by the general public. Let us sketch the nature of the problem. When the allocation of a good or service takes place through a market at a price, any buyer or seller is in principle free to transact any desired quantity in the market. But when the allocation is administered through the CMA – like with defence services – it becomes much more difficult for the individual to make sure that the quantities determined by the CMA are also his desired quantities. This problem of getting what you want out of the CMA applies also to all new laws and regulations that may be enacted by the CMA.

The set of rules and institutions through which the citizens influence the activities of the state (or the CMA) is defined here as the *political system*. It is to the study of the interrelationship between this system and the economic system we now turn.

Theoretically, one could conceive of two extreme variants – in the spirit of the CC and CD models above – through which the general public might influence the activities of the CMA. One would be the situation in which the CMA was left entirely to itself to interpret people's needs and preferences and make the necessary decisions: this political system, where individual participation would be very insignificant, and the degree of centralization of political decision-making high, we may call dictatorship. Diametrically opposite would be the case where each individual decision to be made by the CMA was taken to the general public and voting was performed by everybody involved in the outcome of the decision; this system, where there would be full individual participation in the political process and a high degree of decentralization in political decision-making, we may call democracy.

In real life no societies are 'dictatorships' or 'democracies' in this model sense, but most work with various types of representative government, in which individual participation in political decision-making will differ from problem to problem. To give anything like a satisfactory account of how the political system works at this level in different economic systems is quite impossible here. However, in order to say something on the issue at hand we make the simplifying assumption that the degree of centralization in political decision-making is reflected in the party structure. Thus, a society with a one-party structure will be assumed to be characterized by a higher degree of centralization of political decision-making than one with a multi-party system. For though each country would certainly on closer inspection be found to have a unique party structure, it might still be instructive – as a gross classification – to distinguish between states in which all political influence is concentrated in one party (one-party states) and states in which it is divided among several parties (multi-party states).

Now, if we take the political system defined in this way and the economic system, defined with respect to the importance of state activities, and see how the two aspects are related in real-life societies, it will be found that state activities tend to be more important in one-party states than in multi-party states. How should this be explained?

Is it the one-party structure that tends to create a relatively big role for state activities? Or is it a situation with far-reaching state activity that tends to call forward a one-party structure? Or is there yet a third factor, which causes both the political system and the economic system to occur in the combinations observed?

In the countries where one party dominates all politics and where allocation is highly centralized, i.e. in the Soviet Union and most countries in Eastern Europe, the historical order of causation would certainly seem to have been from a one-party system to a highly centralized economy; the political revolutions came first. But there is a third factor of great importance here, namely that the people in the lead of the dominating party were *ideologically* in favour of a high degree of centralization. Therefore it is difficult to establish, on this approach, to what extent one-party systems *as such* tend to produce much centralization. An illustration of the issue is provided by developments in Nazi Germany, whose leaders were not ideologically biased in favour of centralization in the *economic* field.

Nazi Germany

When the National Socialists came to power in Germany in 1933 the country was quickly transformed from multi-party state into a one-party system, headed by the top officials of the Nazi party. The economic system, predominantly a market economy, was, however, in principle left unchanged.

In 1936 a general price freeze was imposed in Germany. This was because the government had pursued a very active employment policy and created a large surplus of money, which threatened to bring about heavy price rises. The price freeze meant that prices were no longer formed as a result of the interaction of supply and demand on the markets. Consequently prices no longer reflected scarcity values. The longer the price freeze lasted, the less suitable prices became as a basis for different resource allocation decisions. This, together with the heavy demands made on resources by rearmament, led during the late 1930s to an increasing centralization of resource allocation. These tendencies were further reinforced during the war. As resources became scarcer and scarcer, practically all German production decisions were taken centrally.

This is an example of how a decisive change in the political system is likely to lead to changes in the economic system. The centralization of political power gradually led to a centralization of resources allocation decisions.

Alternatively, we may ask if a big role for state activities tends to lead to political system solutions of the one-party type – irrespective of the economic ideologies. In the cases of the Soviet Union and Eastern Europe, the ambitions of the new leaders in terms of accelerated economic growth and redistribution of incomes were so far-reaching that the existing economic system must inevitably come under great pressure to change drastically. Such drastic changes would not be possible in a multi-party system, where the government party or parties lives in the threat always of being thrown out of power if their proposals for changes in the economic system go too far. Through a one-party system, however, it may be possible to organize a political basis for such drastic changes. Similarly, the multi-party system will provide the natural political basis for piece-meal changes in the economic – and political – system.

So far we have considered only why various combinations of political and economic systems might occur, not whether they are likely to remain stable. This complicated issue we can only discuss very briefly here.

In general, it would seem that the two chief types of combinations – those of one-party structure and centralized allocation and of multi-party states and decentralized allocation – are quite stable. The Nazi Germany case cited above is one of the rare instances in developed countries where a multi-party state with a market system has transformed into a one-party state with centralized allocation – without a Communist revolution coming first.

If we look at the other typical combination, i.e. of one-party state and centralized allocation, we find even fewer instances of transformation. The problems that may be incurred in the attempts to make such a transformation are well illustrated by the case of Czechoslovakia.

Czechoslovakia

At the end of the 1950s Czechoslovakia could be described as a one-party state with a centralized economic system. The Communist party was in full control of political life and the economy was directed from Prague.

The economic development of the country stagnated during the early 1960s. National income actually decreased in 1963. The reason was that those in charge of planning had not taken note of the fundamental economic changes undergone by the country. If during the 1950s industry could be made to expand by building up the capital apparatus with 'old' machinery and by means of heavy injections of labour, mostly from agriculture, this was no longer the case by the early 1960s. The reserves of labour were now exhausted and the capital stock therefore had to be improved all the more by means of new techniques, etc., in order to maintain the same growth rate as before.

This was not done. The high degree of centralization in planning did not stimulate local initiatives and proposals for improvements. The leaders of enterprises lacked profitability criteria for any measures that might be taken. At the same time production became increasingly differentiated and information requirements grew accordingly.

At this point several economists and politicians proposed an increased decentralization of economic decision-making so as to utilize the market mechanism on a larger scale. A certain amount of decentralization was introduced in 1967–8. The enterprises were given more freedom of manoeuvre vis-à-vis the CMA. But by no means everybody favoured such 'reforms'. A conflict arose between the 'centralists', led by the party secretary Novotny and other politicians, who were afraid that the proposed decentralization would erode their powers, and the 'decentralists', who wanted to carry the process of decentralization still further. The latter gained the upper hand in the political struggle in 1968 and the decentralization of the economic system was accelerated. But the reform process was abruptly curtailed by the Soviet invasion in August of the same year. Since then the allocation system has become more centralized once again and the Communist party has been further entrenched.

The course of events in Czechoslovakia illustrates well the linkage between the economic and political system. The reforming of the economic system towards decentralization and independence for individual decision-makers freed powers that were thought by many to threaten the traditional one-party structure of the country. The development towards a possible future multi-party state was by many deemed too rapid and uncontrolled. The reaction came with the help of the invasion of the Warsaw Pact forces, and the firm link between a highly centralized economic system and the one dominating Communist party was re-established.

4.2 The Structure of Ownership – an Alternative Approach

As we noted in the introductory chapter, the structure of ownership has often formed the basis of classification in comparative analysis of different economic systems. A system characterized by predominantly private ownership of the means of production has been termed a capitalist system, while a system in which the means of production are owned by the state (or society) is termed socialist.

The basis of classification of economic systems in this book has been the extent to which economic decision-making is decentralized through a market system or centralized to a state authority. Do these two different classification schemes lead to any considerable difference in the analysis of economic systems? Or are the two approaches in fact only two ways of expressing the same phenomenon, meaning for instance that classifying an economy as a decentralized market system must necessarily imply that it can also be characterized as a system with predominantly private ownership, i.e. as a capitalist system?

Ownership: the Legal Aspect – and the Economic

To be able to answer this question we must take a closer look at the concept of ownership, in particular private ownership. It will appear then that the meaning of this concept is much less straightforward than is often believed. But it will also show that, once the concept has been given a certain 'economic' meaning, it becomes very useful for systems analysis, especially of how ownership structure and allocation system hang together.

Now in the language of the law there are clear-cut distinctions between different types of ownership. An asset classified as privately owned is regarded as such by the law as long as it is not officially socialized. This absolute distinction between various types of ownership is, however, not very useful in economic analysis. Think of a (capitalist) economy where ownership is in principle regarded as private but where the original ability of individuals to make use of their ownership rights is considerably attenuated by a series of additional laws. Imagine then a (socialist) economy in which the state has conferred upon private individuals the right to dispose of the means of production in most respects. Although the two systems would be classified as capitalist and socialist, respectively, the difference between them would seem more formal than real.

To get an economically meaningful analysis of the structure of ownership, we therefore have to leave the absolute, legalistic view. Instead, the real nature of ownership should be analysed in terms of the bundle of rights attached to formal ownership. Let us call such rights 'property rights', and determine what property rights should attach to a good to constitute, more strictly, private ownership.

Private Ownership and Market Allocation

Unlimited private ownership is said to be characterized by the exclusive rights of owners to use their property in any way they see fit, including the right to transfer these rights to others. Let us illustrate with the following example. What rights does unlimited private ownership imply for an owner of a multi-dwelling building? According to the definition above it should mean (1) that he can let accommodation at any rent he is willing to accept, (2) that he can dispose of accommodation when a rent contract terminates, let it to any new tenant he prefers or move into it himself, (3) that he can pull the building down and put up a new one, (4) that he can sell the building. The terms of this transfer of rights are determined only by those involved, i.e. buyer and seller, and cannot be imposed on them by a third party, such as the state. Thus, generally speaking, private ownership is unlimited if the individual can do whatever he wants with the property he owns as long as he does not violate the rights of others to use their property.

Now, it will be remembered, in the CD allocation model of chapter 2, that the restrictions on the activities of the state were very similar to those just laid down for unlimited private ownership: the state should help establish general contract laws and react when they were violated, but otherwise let the transfers of property rights (i.e. goods) be determined by buyers and sellers themselves without interference – in what was called markets! We conclude, then, that, with the definition of (unlimited) private ownership chosen here, there is a strong correspondence between allocation system and ownership structure. Indeed, in terms of (the absence of) intervention by the state authorities, decentralized allocation through the market is the twin brother of unlimited private ownership. More generally, it is a *necessary* condition for markets to function that the property rights attached to the good are well defined.

But it is not a *sufficient* condition, for it is also required that the property rights are not too severely circumscribed or restricted by specific laws introduced by the state authorities. Let us return to the case of the landlord to illustrate this aspect. Clearly, in most modern, urbanized economies – in particular in metropolitan areas – there is a great number of tenancy laws that set very definite limits to the 'unlimited' private ownership of the landlord described above. For instance, he may not be able to rent the accommodation at any price he sees fit, for there may be state-administered rent control; or he may not be allowed to pull down his building at his own discretion, for there may be town planning authorities prohibiting this; and so on. Despite the attenuation of many of the property rights in property-owning, there is still a willingness on the part of the landlords to use property right (4), i.e. to buy and sell property. There is a market for accommodation that may still be referred to as 'privately owned', but then it is important to see the economic difference between such private ownership and what we have called unlimited private ownership.

Restricted Private Ownership and Centralized Allocation

Think what would happen if the property rights were even further attenuated. Let us assume, for instance, that it was decreed by the state authorities that a landlord would no longer be allowed to let his property to any tenant he might like, but must choose the tenant most in need (by some agreed-upon social criterion) of accommodation, and assume that it was decreed that no tenant should pay a rent exceeding, say, 5 per cent of his personal earnings – the present rate being, say, 20 per cent. Under these conditions the costs of owning property might no longer be covered by the revenues and the housing market would cease to exist! Allocation must take place instead through the state, according to some criteria set up. This is precisely what has happened with housing allocation in the Soviet economic system.

We see then that, as we move from 'unlimited private ownership' to 'very limited private ownership', allocation tends to become organized by the state rather than through markets. Again, we may speak of the strong correspondence between allocation system and ownership structure: in terms of the far-reaching intervention by state authorities, centralized allocation through the state is the twin brother of very limited private ownership.

Ownership and Allocation in Real Life – Some Illustrations

On the basis of this correspondence between ownership structure and allocation system, we should expect to find real-life economic systems where either market allocation is combined with private ownership or centralized allocation is combined with very limited private ownership ('social' ownership). This, too, is actually what we see in most countries of the world. But there are some instances where the combinations of ownership structure and allocation system seem not to be the expected ones, viz. Yugoslavia and Nazi Germany. How can this be accounted for?

Present-day Yugoslavia is often cited as an example of a combination, where market allocation is combined with a 'socialist' (i.e. non-private) ownership structure. This seeming contradiction – according to our approach – can be dissolved if it is recognized that in most cases what is *formally* termed 'socialist' ownership has *really* turned into private ownership through delegation of decision-making power to individuals (or groups of individuals) so that allocation could take place through markets. In some cases – like with finance capital – it would seem, on the other hand, that what is called 'socialist' ownership really sets very definite limits to market allocation, so that in this area centralized allocation is more likely the actual practice.

Nazi Germany, at the end of the 1930s, is seen as an example of the unlikely combination of centralized allocation with private ownership. Again, the contradiction can be explained if it is recognized that what was here termed 'private ownership' was in reality very far from the unlimited private ownership discussed above. In particular the state had set itself such goals – price stability, heavy increase in armaments, etc. – that they were no longer compatible with the wide property rights of private ownership. Once the state had cut severely into these property rights – demanding that certain goods were delivered by certain firms at certain prices to certain state customers, etc. – it was only natural that market allocation should collapse and state, or central, allocation replace it.

A Summary Conclusion

The answer, then, of the question put at the beginning of this section, of whether classifying economic systems from the point of view of allocation or from the point of view of ownership are only two ways of expressing the same phenomenon, must be in the affirmative. Or, to put it somewhat differently, it makes sense for the economist to work with a definition of private ownership such that it fulfils the requirements of allocation through the market, and with a definition of social ownership such that the allocation must then be handled by the state authorities. In this sense the two points of view are alternative approaches.

4.3 THE CONVERGENCE HYPOTHESIS

In this section we shall describe and examine critically the so-called convergence hypothesis originally suggested (in 1961) by the Dutch economist and Nobel laureate Jan Tinbergen. In his analysis Tinbergen compares the Western capitalist system (represented mainly by the United States) and the Eastern socialist system (represented mainly by the Soviet Union). He finds that the differences between the two economic systems have tended to diminish during the past ten to twenty years. At the same time as economic decision-making has become more decentralized in the socialist states of Eastern Europe, the element of centralized planning has increased in the economies of Western Europe and the United States. And at the same time as interest in the potential advantages of the market systems has increased in the East, the market mechanism has been subjected to growing criticism in the West e.g. in connection with the debate on environmental problems.

These and other observations have led Tinbergen to conclude that the economic systems of the East and the West have moved closer to one another and are still doing so: they are said to be *converging*. According to Tinbergen, this convergence will continue in the future. The economic aspects, like for instance changes in the allocation system, are further said to decide the course of change in society generally. This means that the convergence of the economic systems will be accompanied by a similar convergence in other areas of the society, e.g. the political and the ideological. Eastern socialist and Western capitalist society will come to resemble one another more and more closely.

This is the convergence theory stated in simple terms. More than anything else it is a vision, after a rapid inspection of past developments, of how the future may unfold. But it is not a theory in the scientific sense of the term – at least not in this simplified version – for it leaves too many questions unanswered.

A Critical Examination

The simple version of the convergence theory can be described and criticized in terms of three questions.

First, can one really speak of decentralization and centralization tendencies in the East and the West respectively? There is more than one way of interpreting observations of such complicated relationships as are involved here.

Second: If we none the less are able to confirm that such a development has actually taken place, what can have been the cause of it? There is more than one way of explaining development trends of the kind involved here.

Third: Can these development trends be expected to continue? (Here one is liable to lapse into sheer guesswork.)

More Centralization in the West – More Decentralization in the East?

Has state influence on resource allocation in Western Europe and the United States increased during the postwar period? At the macro-level state economic planning in the West has been increasingly aimed at the maintenance of full employment. Stabilization policy has become more and more active, and can now draw on a wide range of measures of monetary and fiscal policy.

Labour market policy has expanded. More interest has been devoted to regional development policy, and this can partly be seen as an expression of the policy of full employment. In many countries, moreover, considerations of full employment have led national and local authorities to take over the ownership and operation of a large number of enterprises that would otherwise have been closed down.

Gradually, it has been found increasingly necessary for short-term measures of this kind to be supplemented by long-term planning. In many countries alternative economic and social plans are drawn up covering, say, five-year periods. Although these plans have not included any direct orders to enterprises, but have rather provided general information concerning possible development trends, one is still entitled to speak of increased state planning activity.

Another development trend that could be said to have indicated increased centralization in the West is the expansion of the public sector. Medical services and social welfare, education and communications are spheres of public activity that have grown rapidly. The defence sector has also grown rapidly in many countries.

Thus there is some justification for speaking of a certain centralization of economic decision-making in the capitalist Western countries during recent years, but this is a complex phenomenon which cannot be said to have brought about any decisive changes in the decentralized allocation systems that predominate in Western Europe and the United States.

Much the same can be said concerning developments in Eastern Europe. The economic systems of all these countries are more decentralized today than they were in about 1950, but here too we are bound to say that so far no fundamental changes have characterized the allocation system.

Summing up, we can say that the premises of Tinbergen's convergence argument appear reasonable, although neither centralization nor decentralization tendencies are unequivocal. It should be borne in mind, however, that Tinbergen has been concerned with developments from the end of the last war. Had he chosen a starting point further back in time, the resultant picture would have been more equivocal.

Why Centralization in the West and Decentralization in the East?
The centralization tendencies in the West have thus manifested themselves in a number of ways, and for a number of reasons. Political circumstances have played an important part in the steadily rising aspirations of national economic planning for full employment. Since the end of the last war, many countries have had labour governments, while in other countries the labour parties have formed a powerful opposition.

But there are also economic motives behind this increased state activity in the fields of long-term and short-term planning. The need for co-ordination and overall planning has increased in the progressively more complex modern industrial state. As the 'investment packages' of enterprises grow larger, the social consequences of any bad investments that might occur become more and more expensive for the national economy.

The expansion of the public sector is a universal phenomenon. The general rise in welfare standards has meant increasing demands on medical care and social welfare. The expansion of the educational sector and of communications has been a prerequisite for increasing wealth. In all of these cases we are concerned with typical spheres of public activity occasioned by external economies, non-economic considerations, etc.

We have already tried, in the preceding section on economic systems and politics, to account for the decentralization tendencies at work in the Eastern countries, then in the context of Czechoslovakia. A certain decentralization of economic decision-making was suggested by the increased differentiation of consumption requirements and, with them, of production, by increased complexity of central planning and the growing need for information that this entailed. Much the same can be said of developments elsewhere in Eastern Europe since the war. Matters were further complicated in these countries by their (in some cases) extreme dependence on foreign trade.

Will the Convergence Continue?

Of course, it is impossible to give a categorical answer to the question of whether these converging tendencies will continue: the 'equation of the future' contains too many unknowns for that. All we can hope to do is point to different phenomena that can be expected to accelerate or inhibit a development of the kind outlined above, i.e. what Tinbergen has termed a convergence.

First, we have attributed the tendencies towards decentralization in Eastern Europe to the rise in the level of economic development. The more complicated the production process became in the centralized allocation system, the more necessary it was to decentralize decision-making. There is no reason to doubt that the Eastern European economies will continue their rapid development, which would suggest continued decentralization. But then we have not taken into account the possibility of improvements in planning techniques (information processing, computer techniques, etc.), which could instead cause a reversion to more centralized allocation. Nor have we allowed for the eventuality that those who wield the power within the political system may put a stop to any excessive economic decentralization once they feel that their own position is in jeopardy. The case of Czechoslovakia showed the deeply rooted ideological misgivings aroused in Eastern Europe even by the distant threat of a market economy.

Second, the tendencies towards centralization in Western Europe and the United States were said to be connected with changes in the level of economic development and also with political values. Increased demands have been placed on central planning as a means of securing macroeconomic balance, at the same time as there has been a rise in public production for welfare purposes. These tendencies can be expected to continue throughout the foreseeable future: the demands placed on macro-planning can be expected to increase, among other things as a result of increasing interest in growth problems; and the needs that are catered for principally by public production still appear to be far from satisfied. One important but hard-to-foresee factor in this context concerns what social and economic goals will come to determine the future development of the community. This in turn will depend on the development of political values. The same, of course, applies to Eastern Europe.

Tinbergen's 'Optimum Regime'

Tinbergen adopts another approach when assessing the future development of the two systems. Instead of dealing with current development trends and investigating, item by item, the extent to which they can be expected to continue, he concentrates on the question as to which goals of economic policy will be given priority in the future. His contention is that, with the level of economic development rising in East and West alike, these goals will become increasingly similar and will ultimately converge. Tinbergen asserts that each set of goals – be it full employment, a certain stability of prices, a certain well-defined freedom of consumption or whatever – is best achieved by a particular economic system, which he terms 'the optimum regime'.

Since the long-term goals of East and West will be identical, their economic systems will eventually come to be very similar. Tinbergen envisages this optimum regime as a judicious balance between centralization and decentralization of economic decision-making.

As Tinbergen sees it, the convergent tendencies already discernible are connected with this very phenomenon of the increasing similarity of goals of economic policy. At the same time as the Eastern economies have become more and more consumer-oriented, problems of growth have attracted greater interest in the Western countries, and so forth.

Are there no factors outside the economic system that can inhibit development in certain directions (e.g. political obstacles to decentralization in the Eastern countries)? As was hinted in our introduction, Tinbergen's reply to this question is that other factors are conditioned by economic factors, not vice versa. Evidently Tinbergen attaches relatively little significance to the difficult problems of interdependence between the economic system and other aspects of the socio-political environment with which we have been concerned in this chapter.

A Final Comment

Tinbergen's provocative theory can be criticized for its over-emphasis of the importance of economic aspects in the development of society as a whole, for its neglect of certain phenomena and its superficial treatment of others. As we mentioned earlier, our reason for discussing this convergence theory in such detail was that it provided such an excellent illustration of the drastic simplifications and generalizations that have to be made in order to construct anything resembling a theory of how the economic system may be conceived to change when viewed in a broader perspective.

4.4   A DYNAMIC PERSPECTIVE – YUGOSLAVIA IN THE POSTWAR PERIOD*

In chapter 3 the real-life economic systems or the United States and the Soviet Union were presented, each against a background of an idealized model system. Then, in turn, the economic system of France was described against the background of these two real-life systems. In all three cases, the economic ideologies underlying the systems were rather carefully described. But little or nothing was said about all the changes the respective economic systems might have had to go through before they eventually established themselves in the shape described. From a set of ideas of how the economy should ideally be organized, i.e. an economic ideology, to the creation of the actual economic system there is usually a long chain of developments, which will be influenced both by factors in the socio-political environment and by economic development itself. Systems developments in Yugoslavia in the postwar period provide a good illustration of this.

Here the fundamental tenet of the economic ideology was that the economic system should function through enterprises that were managed by the employees themselves – the principle of workers' self-management. At the time – around 1950 – no attempt had ever been made to organize an economic system on similar ideological premises. No wonder, then, that the Yugoslavs were in for many

---

*This section is inspired by the treatment of the Yugoslav economic system in E. Neuberger and W. Duffy, *Comparative Economic Systems: A Decision Making Approach*, Boston, Allen and Bacon, 1976.

surprises and much 'trial and error' when they set out to change their economic system.

One way to describe the Yugoslav effort would be to speak, along Tinbergen's lines, of a search for an 'optimum regime' in terms of allocation arrangements. But the important difference in the Yugoslav case is the introduction of an *a priori* restriction on the system. Only regimes compatible with the principle of workers' self-management can be allowed. As we have already pointed out, Tinbergen denies implicitly the importance of such ideological constraints for the long-run development of economic systems.

The Ideology of Workers' Self-management

It was around 1950 that the political leaders of Yugoslavia set themselves the task of introducing workers' self-management. The motives were twofold: first, to attack the problems of alienation and social conditions in general in the enterprises by giving the workers themselves the necessary powers to manage the enterprise – through some representative voting arrangement; second, and intimately connected with the first, to attack the problems of central coordination through planning and economic inefficiency in general by giving the enterprises themselves greater possibilities to make economic decisions without involving the state authorities.

Clearly, the Yugoslavs had high hopes for their 'own' ideology of self-management: not only would it make enterprises democratic through widespread workers' participation in management, it would also make the whole economy more efficient by decentralizing decision-making. Though this was very different from Soviet ideology, it was in true Marxist spirit, according to the Yugoslavs.

The question was only how these ideological hopes should be interpreted to bear on the actual economic system. What should the new economic system look like? And what were the legacies of the old?

The Yugoslav Economy Around 1950

Five years after the Second World War, Yugoslavia still had a fairly undeveloped agrarian-type economy. It was also a strongly centrally planned economy on Soviet principles, though this applied mainly to the less developed industrial sector. A central administrative apparatus had been set up, which operated the enterprises through detailed instructions. As a result prices had no allocative functions; neither did private ownership of enterprise capital, which had been socialized when the Communists under Marshall Tito had established themselves as the one leading party.

Self-management – Through What Economic System?

Of the two motives of self-management, 'enterprise democracy' and 'systemic efficiency', the former was for obvious reasons much more easily fitted into an organizational framework than the latter. The right to make economic decisions was vested in the workers' collective, which would typically elect among themselves a workers' council of between 15 and 120 members to decide on important issues in production (output targets, etc.). This body would be too cumbersome to handle current affairs, and so a smaller management group has been organized by the workers' council to take care of this. On this representative model of 'enterprise democracy' there seems to have been little disagreement, when the law was formally passed in 1950.

Much more complicated was the determination of what exactly should be the 'decision domain' for the workers' council, i.e. of the enterprise relative to the state authorities, to ensure 'systemic efficiency'. Should Yugoslavia go all the way and give individual enterprises the right to decide what to produce and how, how much to export and import, whether to expand or reduce capacities or, indeed, to establish new factories? A solution along such lines would imply that most of the co-ordination of the enterprises' decision would have to be through markets, and no longer through the CMA. Now to make decentralization viable, well-functioning competitive markets are needed. Otherwise prices will not reflect scarcity values and cannot be used as the basis for co-ordinating economic decisions. And for the enterprises really to be able to influence investment decisions they must have access to financial capital independently of the CMA, through retained profits or through organized credit and capital markets. So, in addition, the CMA would have to divest itself of its command over both prices and investment allocations to make such a decentralized market solution possible.

If such full-scale decentralization was ever considered among the architects of the new economic system we do not know. It would seem to be a good guess, however, that if it had been it would have had very little chance of being accepted, in particular by the people involved in planning. Think of all the efforts invested by planning officers to achieve a functioning hierarchy; most of them would oppose any decentralization from the CMA to the market. And think of all the millions of visible and invisible links established between planners, managers and workers under the old centrally planned economy; whatever hopes were pinned on a new system, there would always be an element of insecurity in moving away from the old rules-of-the-game. And, last but not least, think of the basic ideological frame of reference of the political leaders; negatively tuned toward market allocation and decentralization in general, they would most likely prefer not-so-decentralized solutions.

Also, the new economic system launched in the early 1950s to accommodate self-management was very much an incidental combination of old and new. The CMA let go of price control in some areas but not in others. Direct central planning with detail instructions to the enterprises was largely discontinued. Instead, enterprises were to work for profit, but in the rather special sense this concept takes on when enterprise investments are financed through centralized funds rather than own profits. Similarly with respect to foreign trade: some enterprises involved in trade were allowed to deal in foreign currency, others are not.

Ten Years Later

It did not take long to show that the 'first' economic system was by no means the 'optimum regime'. Around 1960 the situation became directly critical and new rules were suggested. There were several reasons why the system did not work well. The fundamental problem was to organize or time the transition from a highly centralized allocation system to a relatively decentralized system in such a way that, when central co-ordinating instructions were no longer forthcoming, they would be immediately replaced by other signals, i.e. market prices. In Yugoslavia it would seem that direct planning was discontinued too quickly for alternative markets to have time to establish themselves in an orderly way. This problem was further aggravated by the many prices that survived from the old system and that did not reflect actual social costs. Furthermore, heavy restrictions on foreign trade tended to give Yugoslav enterprises monopoly advantages and to weaken competition.

Another problem, already hinted at above, had to do with the fact that the state authorities preferred to generate funds for enterprise investments through central allocation rather than through enterprise profits. As a result, the workers' collective felt little incentive to innovate, reduce costs, etc., as a means to increase profits and thereby future investment opportunities for itself.

There were also problems more directly related to workers' self-management within enterprises. Here, the decentralization of the employment decision to the individual enterprises – i.e. the workers' council – had produced a number of cases where equal work was given very different payment in different enterprises because of differences in starting conditions and because of the unwillingness of high-income enterprises to employ more people. Such practices have caused both resentment and efficiency losses (through low labour mobility). But it was never seriously suggested that the ideal of workers' self-management should be abandoned.

Remodelling the Economic System Once Again

In this situation the system designers had to decide whether they should go on decentralizing the economy, accepting the conditions necessary for a functioning market system, or return to the old system of rigid central planning.

The decision, eventually, was to try decentralization. But this was by no means the evident choice. Indeed, in the first half of the 1960s Yugoslavia was troubled by a more or less continuous struggle between 'centralists' and 'decentralists' about the future economic system. This struggle was not primarily one between centralist old planners, who saw an opportunity to get back in power in an expanded CMA, and decentralist managers (and workers), who wanted to widen even further their growing 'decision domain'. Neither was it a fight between conservative planners and managers, on the one hand, and the Communist Party on the other. Instead, the core of the conflict was within the party itself! The chief opponent to President Tito's decentralist line was Alexander Rankovic. Rankovic, who was a moderate centralist, was for a number of years in a position to obstruct attempts at decentralization, and so it was not until he and his group of 'vested interest opponents' had left office (in 1966) that the 'second' economic system could be tried out seriously.

The new system was specifically designed to do away with the insufficiencies of the old. Very few prices were now left directly to the discretion of the CMA. To make sure that prices give a reasonable reflection of social costs, they were realigned with relative prices in the world market. Once prices had been improved as allocation signals, the next step was to increase the enterprises' incentive to act according to these signals by allowing them to retain – and dispose of – a fair share of their revenues (profits). To strengthen competition, protectionist measures were removed and Yugoslav firms became exposed to the competitive conditions in the world market.

Self-management and the Economic System Today

The 'second' economic system, introduced in the middle of the 1960s, has not been free of problems, either. There has been both inflation and unemployment on a fairly large scale. But efficiency has probably improved, and so the present economic system could perhaps be described as a 'tolerable', although far from 'optimum', regime.

It is not clear how decentralized the Yugoslav economic system of today is. So much is still unknown – or invisible – to the outside observer of all CMA activities that an overall picture is difficult to discern. It is sometimes suggested that the Yugoslav economic system of today is at least as decentralized as that of France – which seems reasonable as long as we talk about current decisions about production. It is less true when we talk about investment decisions, because of the absence of a decentralized capital market, and even less true concerning the entry of new firms.

To what extent could the ideology of workers' self-management be thought to have been the actual cause of this high degree of decentralization? A more centralized allocation system might also have been compatible with self-management as a principle *within* the enterprise. Could it be that there is a link here between *how* allocation decisions are made within the enterprise and *what* these decisions should concern (meaning for instance that it would not make sense *first* to give the workers' collective the power to decide within the enterprise and *then* reduce its value to nothing by running the whole economy through a CMA)? Such questions point to the need to investigate further the organization of micro-units in the study of economic systems.

5. Evaluating and Comparing Economic Systems

One reason for studying economic systems is to try and find which is the best one. To do this, it is necessary first to evaluate the performance of different systems and then to compare the values ascribed to each system. Some problems involved in such comparisons are discussed in the second section of this chapter, where it is also emphasized how difficult it is to draw a clear line of causation from economic (or allocation) system to economic performance.

Given the importance of the economic system for the material and other well-being of people, one might have guessed that evaluating and comparing economic systems is already a well-developed field of study in economics. It is not. It is probably fair to say that it has begun to develop only in the last decade or so. Before then the comparison of economic systems was in large part a matter either of presenting and disputing blueprint systems or of making sheer propaganda. A short review of this 'pre-history' of systems comparisons will be given in the first section of the chapter. The purpose of this review is to call attention to some of the false simplifications one is liable to make when undertaking evaluative comparisons of different economic systems.

5.1   A SHORT HISTORY OF ECONOMIC SYSTEMS ANALYSIS

The Early Debate – Much Belief and Little Realism

The debate on economic systems was not particularly lively at the turn of the century, a time when, both in Europe and the United States, the current system was taken for granted as the best conceivable one. The industrial revolution had got underway in large portions of these parts of the world, and rapid economic advance was pre-eminently associated with the independent, industrious entrepreneur. It was regarded as self-evident that the means of production should be privately owned in order for personal ability to come into its own. Most people at this time simply could not imagine the possibility of any system other than the decentralized market economy with private ownership, i.e. the system sometimes referred to as private capitalism.

This is not to say that the capitalist economic system was free from criticism during the nineteenth century. Mention can be made here of the so-called Utopian socialists (Proudhon, Fourier and others) and, of course, Marx. The criticism put forward was often vehemently anti-capitalist, but few properly worked-out alternatives were offered.

The early years of the present century, however, saw the beginning of a debate on the socialist economy in which a real attempt was made to formulate such alternatives. This debate, which attained its peak in the 1930s, was concerned above all with the question whether a 'socialist' economy, i.e. an economy in which allocation decisions were largely centralized, might work satisfactorily. The Austrian economist Friedrich Hayek maintained that, although a centrally planned socialist economy might very well function, it could not be expected to do so efficiently in view of the overwhelming problems of information that would arise. Hayek regarded the decentralized market economy as the best system alternative in terms of efficiency.

Not long afterwards (in 1938), the Polish economist Oskar Lange tried to show that the price system, so vital to co-ordinate allocation decisions in the market economy, could very well be utilized also as an aid in co-ordination in a socialist economy. If only the managers of the enterprises were instructed on how to translate the market-simulated price signals by the CMA into production decisions, co-ordination would be no problem. This scheme, Lange asserted, would function even if the equity capital of the enterprises was owned and managed by the state. Indeed, this economic system would be superior to the 'capitalist' market economy, since here the market would be supplemented through a strong CMA with an overview of the whole economy that was missing in the capitalist economy. Lange's model is usually referred to as the 'socialist market model'. This is misleading, for reasons developed in section 4.2 above. Lange's model is a combination of allocation through markets (final goods, intermediate goods) and through the state (financial capital – which may be said to be state-owned or 'socialist').

Finally, there were economists who, for various reasons, advocated systems of centralized resource allocation (and state ownership) more along the lines of the Soviet economic system (Dobb, Sweezy).

At the same time as it served to define the basic concepts of economic systems, this whole debate was remarkably theoretical. One is struck by the very few examples that were quoted from the experiment with a socialist planned economy then actually in progress in the Soviet Union. The debate, known as 'the socialist controversy', was so concerned with theoretical models that the conclusions arrived at concerning the most efficient system were hardly applicable to the mixed economies of real life.

The Later Debate – Much Statistics and Little Analysis

If the socialist controversy was concerned mainly with comparisons of theoretical systems, the opposite applies to the 'comparative systems debate' that took place above all in the 1950s. The question now was which system, the Soviet or the American, possessed the greater productive capacity. In evaluating these two systems, however, attention was exclusively concentrated on comparing the current achievements of the two countries in different sectors of special political and economic importance. Individual sectors, e.g. coal and steel production, military industrial potential, space exploration achievements, etc., were selected for purposes of comparison, but there existed no analytical framework through which such comparisons could be made to give any useful information about the economic systems of the two economies.

Nor was very much allowance made for the completely different historical backgrounds of the Soviet Union and the United States or for their different levels of economic development. The United States in the 1950s had long been a fully developed industrial nation. The Soviet Union, on the other hand, after violent efforts during the 1930s, built up an impressive heavy industrial sector while at the same time other sectors, e.g. agriculture and consumer goods, were still fairly underdeveloped. Also, while the market system had been in operation for hundreds of years, the experiment with the planned economy had only just started.

One frequent mistake, particularly in comparisons of the economic systems of the Soviet Union and the United States, has been to compare the real-life workings of one country with an idealized notion of the other. Both Americans and Russians have been guilty of simplifications of this kind, and the resultant comparisons are of no use to anybody except the propagandist.

5.2   WHICH SYSTEM IS THE BEST?

The most difficult problem when evaluating and comparing different economic systems lies in defining what one means by saying that one system is 'better' than another. Not surprisingly, most people have different opinions on this point. An economic system includes too many dimensions for a single criterion – on which everybody can agree – to suffice. Instead we have to use a set of criteria giving as comprehensive a picture as possible of the qualities of the economic system. But these criteria should also, preferably, be universal and accepted by as many people as possible. To give an example, many Americans would regard the right to conduct business activities as a criterion of the satisfactory functioning of an economic system. This is not surprising when seen in its historical context. Earlier we saw how the rapid economic development of the United States during the nineteenth century was associated by the majority of Americans with the liberal economic policy which gave full rein to individual initiative. Eventually this entrepreneurial freedom came to be regarded as an end in itself rather than a means of achieving rapid economic growth. To the majority of Russians, to take another example, entrepreneurial freedom of this kind would be unacceptable for ideological reasons. Consequently, if we wish to state criteria which will be acceptable to all, entrepreneurial freedom will not be among them.

Criteria for Evaluation – a Suggestion

In this section we propose a list of criteria that seem to be generally acceptable and that cover fairly broadly the various aspects of performance of an economic system. To get an aggregate evaluation of an economic system's performance it is further necessary to have some kind of welfare function according to which the different criteria can be given appropriate weights. These weighting problems will be dealt with below.

The criteria* that we propose are the following:
(1) level of output;
(2) rate of growth of output;
(3) composition of output (the shares of consumption, investment and military programmes; collective v. individual consumption);
(4) efficiency;
(5) stability (of output, employment, prices);
(6) equity and economic security of the individual;
(7) adaptability to change.

Before going into a discussion of each of these criteria, we note that some of them are complementary, i.e. mutually reinforcing; for example, a high degree of stability in employment and prices would imply increased economic security for the individual. Others may be competitive, i.e. mutually conflicting; for instance, a high rate of growth may be in conflict with a 'fair' distribution of income and wealth.

Criteria 1–3 need few comments. Few would deny that it would be desirable *per se* to have a high level of output and high rate of growth of this output. But too strong emphasis on building up the capital stock and military potential would not be desirable, since the ultimate aim would still in every economic system be to increase the standard of living of the individual consumers. Thus the importance of adding criterion (3), the composition of output.

---

*This discussion on the choice of appropriate criteria draws on the treatment given in an article 'Description and Comparison of Economic Systems' (in *Comparison of Economic Systems*. edited by A. Eckstein, University of California Press, Berkeley 1971) written by the Nobel Laureate Tjalling Koopmans and John Montias.

Criterion (4), efficiency, has a character somewhat different from the first three. While the level, growth and composition of output are all fairly easily measurable, efficiency is a more abstract concept and therefore more difficult to measure. The efficiency criterion could be said to be complementary to criteria 1–3, in the sense that the pursuit of these criteria will also imply the pursuit of efficiency in the use of resources.

Efficiency is a concept of strategic importance in economic analysis and has consequently been given a rigorous definition. Perfect efficiency of an economy is defined as the choice of production activities such that, within the limits of the given resource availabilities, it is not technologically possible to produce more of any good without producing less of some other good. In other words, the economy is on its production possibility frontier. If we further add the assumption that consumers' preferences are to count, we get an extended definition of efficiency often termed Pareto optimality: perfect efficiency or Pareto optimality is attained when it is not possible to increase the well-being of any individual without decreasing that of another.

Efficiency defined this way is a perfectly general concept, applicable to all conceivable economic systems. There is, however, a tendency to associate discussions about efficiency mainly with the analysis of *market* economies. This is probably so because economic theory has established an interesting link between the market system and the concept of efficiency. Under certain (fairly restrictive) conditions it is possible to show that a completely decentralized market economy will automatically and without any interventions satisfy the requirements for perfect efficiency and Pareto optimality. In fact, this finding is considered one of the most important achievements of economic analysis and provides the basis for most studies of the workings of market economies. The intuitive reasoning in the chapter 2 presentation of the CD model is thus based on more rigorous analysis. For example, the contention that, in the ideal world of the model market, prices will convey perfect information about relative scarcities in the economy is given a rigorous meaning in this analysis. This connection between efficiency and the *ideal* model of a market system does not allow us, however, to draw the conclusion that *actually existing* market economies must inevitably be superior to centrally planned economies with respect to efficiency. This is a proposition that can be vindicated only by empirical studies.

It is fruitful to distinguish between *single-period* and *intertemporal* efficiency. Single-period – or static – efficiency obtains if all the inputs and outputs in the definition refer to one single time period. Capital stocks and technology are treated as given, inherited from the past. According to the definition, perfect single-period efficiency may be obtained in every period, even in a stationary economy with no growth. Intertemporal – or dynamic – efficiency usually refers to the optimal choice between consumption and saving over time, i.e. the optimal rate of capital accumulation. It may also be extended to include the capacity of a system to discover and exploit new techniques, and to develop and introduce new products. Especially with this broader meaning, intertemporal efficiency becomes a very complex motion with no generally agreed-upon definition. This explains why efficiency discussions usually deal only with the single-period aspect, although the intertemporal aspect is probably the more interesting one. Attempts at numerical evaluations of efficiency consequently have largely used the definition of single-period efficiency as their point of reference.

Criterion (5), stability of employment, income and prices, is also a fairly obvious one. The fight against unemployment and inflation has long been a matter of major concern for the governments in the industrialized market economies. Unless unemployment and inflation figures are kept below some tolerable levels, the whole working of the market system is threatened. The German hyperinflation in the 1920s and the Great Depression in the United States and Europe in the 1930s are warning examples from history. In centrally planned economies these problems are much less severe. At least according to the official statistics, unemployment and inflation of the general price level hardly exist. Instead, these economies seem to have problems with instability in the production of physical output. Errors in planning may have cumulative effects leading to heavy swings in, for instance, inventory production.

The concern with distribution among individuals is expressed by criterion (6). Equity, like efficiency, is an abstract concept, but there is no generally accepted definition of perfect or optimal equity as was the case with efficiency. We have to be content with discussing equity somewhat loosely in terms of 'appropriate' degrees of equality in income and wealth, or more generally in the conditions of living, including opportunities to education and employment, protection against the effects of accidents and bad health, absence of racial and similar kinds of discrimination, etc.

The last criterion, (7), may seem less obvious than the others. Adaptability to change is, however, probably a very important characteristic of an economic system. If there are no well-developed mechanisms in the system that helps it adjust to changing circumstances without endangering the basic working of the system, the economy will either become stagnant within an obsolete institutional framework or be hit by abrupt changes of a revolutionary character. A provision for orderly change in a system thus seems to be generally desirable.

How Should the Different Criteria Be Weighed Together?

If the criteria presented above are accepted as giving a broad cover of the various performance aspects of an economic system and we succeed in getting approximate numerical values on them, there still remains the task of finding an appropriate weight distribution or welfare function. Unless, in a comparison of two economic systems, one country displays superior performance according to *all* criteria, no ranking of the systems is possible without assigning appropriate weights to the different criteria. It is conceivable, for instance, that one of the countries has concentrated heavily on rapid economic growth and has paid less attention to equity and efficiency. The other country, on the other hand, may have emphasized equity and attached less importance to growth. Expressed in terms of a weight distribution or welfare function this would indicate that growth got relatively larger weight and equity and efficiency relatively smaller weight in the welfare function of the first country, and that the converse would be true for the second country, i.e. a relatively large weight for equity and a small weight for growth. With these weights established it is possible to obtain an overall measure or index of the performance of the two economies as a weighted sum of the values achieved for each criterion.

Who determines the distribution of these weights? In other words, who determines that, for instance, growth is to be regarded as a relatively more important objective than, say, equity? Obviously what we want to know is who determines ultimately the goals, economic and political, of society. Two extremes are conceivable. In one case the objectives of society are entirely determined according to the desires of the individual members of the society; i.e., the weights are determined in a *pluralistic* way. In the opposite case the weights are set exclusively by the state authorities. The state may be a benevolent one, trying to follow what it considers to be a true reflection of the desires of the individual citizens; or it may, at least in principle, choose to disregard them altogether. This way of determining the weight distribution is called *paternalistic*.

None of these extremes is to be found in reality. In all countries the goals of society are determined through the interaction of the preferences of the individuals as expressed in the market (and in the ballot-box) and the objectives of those executing the power of government.

A Laboratory Experiment

If one succeeded in making a scientifically acceptable evaluation of the economic performance of various countries, along the lines sketched above, this would obviously be an important and useful achievement. We would probably not, however, have provided enough information to answer the question posed in the beginning of this chapter, i.e. we are not yet in a position to judge whether one type of *economic system* is superior to another. How does one have to proceed to be able to make such statement?

In chapter 4 we discussed various factors, the political system, the size and geographical location, etc., that interact with the economic system in the determination of the actual economic performance of a country. To be able to explain the superior performance during a certain time period of a country with, say, predominantly market allocation compared with another country with a strongly centralized economy by referring to its specific choice of economic system, these other factors must have been very similar in the two countries during the period of comparison. Otherwise we cannot be certain that the choice of economic system has been the decisive factor behind the difference in performance. The different choice of political system or the different location of the country might as well have been the main contributing factor.

To illustrate this we may think of the following 'laboratory' experiment. Suppose we could find two countries, which at a particular point in time, say thirty years ago, were at the same level of development, shared a similar historical background, had a similar size and location, in short had very similar initial conditions. At this time the two countries choose two fundamentally different economic systems. During the ensuing thirty years they are not subjected to any considerably different external influences such as wars or other disasters. When the thirty years are up the economic performance of the two countries over the period is compared. If it then turns out that one country gets a superior record, one can attribute this achievement to the choice of a better economic system.

In real life such 'laboratory' experiments are of course impossible to perform in a strict sense. But although such ideal cases are missing, we may still make country comparisons that fulfil the norms to a fair extent. Thus East and West Germany or Greece and Yugoslavia during the postwar period could provide a fruitful basis for such a comparative study.*

---

*Such studies have in fact been done; see for instance M. Schnitzer, *East and West Germany: A Comparative Economic Analysis*, Praeger, New York (1972), and B. Ward, 'Capitalism vs. Socialism: A Small Country Version' in G. Grossman (ed.), *Essays in Socialism and Planning in Honor of Carl Landauer*, Prentice-Hall, Englewood Cliffs, N.J. (1970).

Suggestions for Further Reading

There are few analytically satisfactory textbooks on comparative economic systems. A shining exception is provided by E. Neuberger and W. Duffy, *Comparative Economic Systems: A Decision-Making Approach*, Allyn and Bacon, Boston (1976). It is more detailed and more advanced than this book but is still simple enough to be read by the non-specialist. For advanced treatments written for professional economists see A. Eckstein (ed.), *Comparison of Economic Systems. Theoretical and Methodological Approaches*, University of California Press, Berkeley (1971) and J. M. Montias, *The Structure of Economic Systems*, Yale University Press, New Haven (1976). Useful books of readings are M. Bornstein, *Comparative Economic Systems. Models and Cases*, Richard D. Irwin, Homewood, Ill. (1969) and J. Prybyla, *Comparative Economic Systems*, Appleton-Century-Crofts, New York (1969).

Of the theoretical models presented in chapter 2 the CD model is of course the basic model presented in all elementary courses in allocation theory. R. Dorfman, *The Price System*, Prentice Hall, Englewood Cliffs, New Jersey (1964); F. M. Bator, 'The Simple Analytics of Welfare Maximization', *American Economic Review* (March 1957) and P. Bohm, *Social Efficiency. A Concise Introduction to Welfare Economics*, Macmillan, London (1974) provide good introductions to the theory of the market economy. For attempts at establishing a theoretical framework for the centrally planned economy see E. Neuberger, 'Libermanism, Computopia and Visible Hand. The Question of Informational Efficiency', *American Economic Review* (May 1966) and P. Pelikan, 'Language as a Limiting Factor for Centralization', *American Economic Review* (September 1969). The classic and still extremely readable treatment of the information aspect of economic systems is found in F. A. Hayek, 'The Use of Knowledge in Society', *American Economic Review* (reprinted in Bornstein, op. cit).

With reference to chapter 3, a comprehensive description of the structure of the American economy is given in R. Caves, *American Industry:*

Structure, Conduct, Performance, Prentice Hall, Englewood Cliffs, NJ (1967). The public sector in the United States is studied in detail in O. Eckstein, *Public Finance*, Prentice Hall, Englewood Cliffs, NJ (1965). Two elegant surveys of the American economic system with widely differing views are provided by M. Friedman, *Capitalism and Freedom*, University of Chicago Press, (1962) and J. K. Galbraith, *American Capitalism: The Concept of Countervailing Power*, Houghton Mifflin, Boston (1957). For an elementary survey of 'market failures' in general, see F. M. Bator, 'The Anatomy of Market Failure', *Quarterly Journal of Economics* (August 1958).

The most comprehensive introduction to the Soviet economic system is provided by A. Nove, *The Soviet Economy: An Introduction*, Praeger, New York (1977). A less detailed but quite satisfactory alternative is R. W. Campbell, *Soviet-Type Economies*, Macmillan, London (1974). Two short articles by R. W. Davies, 'The Soviet Planning Process for Rapid Industrialization' and 'Planning in a Mature Economy in the USSR', both in *Economics of Planning* (1966) (reprinted in Prybyla, op. cit.), give a surprisingly comprehensive introduction to the Soviet economy. For a detailed and interesting description of Soviet economic history, see A. Nove, *An Economic History of the USSR*, Penguin, Harmondsworth (1969).

A comprehensive treatment of the French economic system and in particular of French planning is found in V. Lutz, *Central Planning for the Market Economy: An Analysis of the French Theory and Experience*, Longmans, London (1969). Another valuable discussion on French planning is given in B. Balassa, 'Whither French Planning?', *Quarterly Journal of Economics* (November 1965). I. Svennilson, *Planning in a Market Economy*, Weltwirtschaftliches Archiv (1965), contains a general discussion of economic planning in market economies.

For chapter 4, an introduction to the analysis of political systems is given in R. A. Dahl, *Modern Political Analysis*, Prentice Hall, Englewood Cliffs, NJ (1963). For further study of the 'property rights' approach to allocation theory see E. Furubotn and S. Pejovich (eds.), *The Economics of Property Rights*, Ballinger, Cambridge, Mass. (1974) (especially the articles by Demsetz, Alchian and Nutter) and the brilliant textbook by A. Alchian and W. Allen, *University Economics. Elements of Inquiry*, Wadsworth, Belmont, California (1972), (especially chapter 9).

The classic treatment of the economic system of Nazi Germany is W. Eucken, 'On the Theory of the Centrally Administered Economy: An Analysis of the German Experiment', *Economica* (May and August 1948) (reprinted in Bornstein, op. cit.).

The original article presenting the convergence hypothesis is J. Tinbergen, 'Do Communist and Free Economies show a Converging Pattern?', *Soviet Studies* (April 1961) (reprinted in Bornstein, op. cit.). Another valuable discussion is found in J. Prybyla, 'Convergence of Market-Oriented and Command-Oriented Systems: A Critical Estimate', *The Russian Review* (January 1964) (reprinted in Prybyla, op. cit.).

An elegant survey of the development of the Yugoslav economic system is found in Neuberger and Duffy, op. cit., chapter 15. In E. Neuberger and E.

James, 'The Yugoslav Self-Managed Enterprise' in M. Bornstein (ed.), *Plan and Market: Economic Reform in Eastern Europe*, Yale University Press, New Haven (1973), a penetrating analysis of the system of workers' self-management is presented.

In conjunction with chapter 5, the socialist controversy is neatly summarized in B. Ward, *The Socialist Economy: A Study of Organizational Alternatives*, Random House, New York (1967). For general discussions about the problems of comparative evaluations and suggestions for the choice of appropriate performance criteria see T. Koopmans and J. M. Montias, 'On the Description and Comparison of Economic Systems', in Eckstein, op. cit., and B. Balassa, 'Success Indicators for Economic Systems', in *The Hungarian Experience in Economic Planning*, Yale University Press, New Haven (1959) (reprinted in Bornstein, op. cit.).

Glossary

ACCOUNTING PRICES: prices serving the sole purpose of making different goods additive, where no information requirements are placed on the sum other than that it be a sum.

AMALGAMATION: merger between firms.

AGGREGATE (economic): aggregates are totals of individual units; e.g., the aggregate consumption in an economy is the total consumption of all individual households added together.

ALLOCATION (of resources): the process of deciding what inputs should go to what firms or sectors of production, and which outputs should be distributed to which consumers.

ANTI-TRUST LEGISLATION: the set of laws through which central government tries to fight the tendencies towards cartelization and monopolization in the business sector.

CAPITAL STOCK: the amount of physical, real capital at a point in time.

CAPITALIST ECONOMY: an economy in which the means of production are owned – predominantly – by private individuals.

CARTEL: an agreement between sellers (or buyers) serving to limit mutual competition in price, quality, etc.

CC MODEL: the idealized model of completely centralized allocation (through a CMA).

CD MODEL: the idealized model of completely decentralized allocation (through markets).

CENTRAL MACRO-LEVEL AUTHORITY (CMA): the agency for economic decisions at the government level.

CENTRALIZED ALLOCATION: the process by which all decisions about what should be consumed, invested and produced are made by one central body.

104

COLLECTIVE GOOD: a good the consumption of which non-buyers cannot be excluded from.

CONCENTRATION (of firms): number of producers in an industry: the smaller the number, the higher is the degree of concentration in production.

CONSENSUS (PERFECT) OF VALUES: situation in which (1) 'producers and consumers do not wilfully mislead the decision-makers in the CMA'; (2) 'consumers and producers . . . fulfil . . . the decisions of the CMA to the best of their ability'.

CONSISTENCY: (1) of a plan: 'all foreseen needs of goods and services fit in exactly with a corresponding set of centrally decided deliveries with no resources left over or missing'; (2) in the market: all firms and households who want to transact goods or labour can do so without facing situations of excess supply or demand in the markets.

COST-PLUS-PRICES: prices based on average unit production cost plus a mark-up (according to some rule).

DECENTRALIZED ALLOCATION: the process by which all decisions about what should be consumed, invested and produced are made by the households and firms themselves.

DIRECT CENTRAL PLANNING: central planning of the Soviet type, whereby orders are laid down directly to enterprises.

ECONOMIC SYSTEM: 'the network of institutions and arrangements directed towards economizing the scarce resources of a certain organization'. This organization can be a business enterprise, a national state, or, indeed, the whole world.

ECONOMIES OF SCALE: situation occurring when the unit (average) cost of production decreases as the scale of production increases.

EFFICIENCY: 'the choice of production activities such that within the limits of the given resources availabilities it is not technologically possible to produce more of any good without producing less of some other good'.

ENTREPRENEUR: businessmen, in particular those who start new business or introduce new products or techniques.

EQUILIBRIUM (price): situation in which all in the market who want to buy and sell at the equilibrium price can do so, without any sellers getting any unsold goods left or any buyers not getting the goods they demand.

EXCESS DEMAND: demand for a quantity at a certain price greater than the quantity supplied at that price.

EXCESS SUPPLY: supply of a quantity at a certain price greater than the quantity demanded at that price.

EXTERNAL ECONOMIES (diseconomies): when the activity of an individual household or firm produces gains (losses) for other households or firms without this being reflected in market prices.

EXTERNALITIES: see EXTERNAL ECONOMIES (DISECONOMIES).

FISCAL POLICY: measures taken by central government, typically involving tax rates and public expenditure, to secure economic stability.

GOSPLAN: the state planning committee of the Soviet Union, which is the top central co-ordinator of economic planning.

INCOME DISTRIBUTION: the distribution of national income among individuals, households, factors of production or according to other schemes of classification.

INDICATIVE PLANNING: central planning of the French type, where plans indicate future economic development, but where direct instructions are not given to the enterprises.

INDIRECT CENTRAL PLANNING: central planning of the US type, where orders are *not* laid down directly to enterprises; instead – to secure economic stability – central economic policy seeks to affect enterprises indirectly through general economic measures.

INPUT-OUTPUT COEFFICIENT (norm): a number describing the (maximum) use of an input (e.g. raw materials, semi-fabricates) per unit of output.

INTERDEPENDENCE: mutual dependence between two or more factors (like prices in markets for neighbouring goods, the economic system and the political system, etc.).

KOLKHOZ MARKET: a local, decentralized market for agricultural goods produced by *kolkhoz* people (and other owners of private plots in the USSR).

MARGINAL COSTS: the increase in the total cost of production when production increases by one unit.

MATERIAL BALANCE: summary statement of the targeted needs and supplies of individual goods.

MICRO-UNIT: firms and households are micro-units, i.e. units of analysis at the micro-level, where the national aggregate of firms and households has been disaggregated to individual units in separate markets.

MONETARY POLICY: measures taken by the central bank (government) to secure economic stability, typically involving interest rates and the supply of credits in the capital market.

NATIONAL INCOME: the value of the total production of goods and services in a country (over a certain period of time), net of all 'double-counted' inputs.

NATIONAL PRODUCT: (1) gross: the value of the total national production of goods and services (over a certain period of time), net of all 'double-counted' inputs, but including gross investments (GNP): (2) net: GNP minus the value of replacement investments (NNP).

NATURAL MONOPOLY: when economies of scale are so great that it would be wasteful for society not to concentrate production on one single enterprise.

OLIGOPOLY: a market in which relatively few big firms dominate (and watch each other's behaviour).

PARETO OPTIMALITY: 'when it is not possible to increase the well-being of any individual without decreasing that of another'.

PLAN (economic): a programme for or a set of instructions for future action, laying down – in varying degree of detail – what should be produced and how, and at what level of the enterprise (or the nation).

PLAN INDICATOR: a reward-related plan instruction through which the CMA tries to ensure that managers' decisions are in accordance with the intentions of the CMA.

PLANNING: 'a process of preparing decisions for action in the future'.

POLITICAL SYSTEM: the set of rules and institutions through which the citizens influence the activities of the state.

PRICE-TAKER: a firm or household that views the market price as a given, which cannot be affected through measures of his own.

PROPERTY RIGHTS: the bundle of rights — to sell, to whom, etc. — attached to formal ownership.

RESTRICTIVE TRADE PRACTICES: measures taken by buyers or sellers in a market designed to restrain competition in terms of price, quality, channels of distribution, etc.

SCARCITY PRICES: prices describing the relative scarcity of different goods; such prices may be observable market prices or 'non-observable' shadow prices computed centrally.

SHADOW PRICES: prices computed by the planners describing the (scarcity) value of an additional unit of a good in short supply.

SOCIAL COST: the total cost to society of choosing a production alternative; this cost may be exaggerated where monopoly power is exerted and underestimated where there are negative external economies.

SOCIALIST ECONOMY: an economy in which the means of production are owned – predominantly – by collectives of individuals, in particular the state.

STABILIZATION POLICY: measures taken by central government to secure a (high and) stable rate of capacity utilization, in particular of labour (full employment), and a (low and) stable rate of inflation; such measures will be monetary or fiscal policy measures.

TRANSFER PAYMENTS: redistribution of money through (central) government primarily to households.

WELFARE FUNCTION: a distribution of weights ascribed to various criteria of performance – e.g. efficiency, equity – of an economic system.

WORKERS' COUNCIL: the chief decision-making body in Yugoslav enterprises, elected by the collective of workers.

Index